D0855858

Development of Species Identification in Birds

WAYNE J. ARENDT

Development of Species Identification in Birds

An Inquiry into the Prenatal Determinants of Perception

Gilbert Gottlieb

THE UNIVERSITY OF CHICAGO PRESS
CHICAGO AND LONDON

International Standard Book Number: 0-226-30505-8
Library of Congress Catalog Card Number: 76-128712

The University of Chicago Press, Chicago 60637
The University of Chicago Press, Ltd., London

Printed in the United States of America

To the memory of ZING-YANG KUO, 1898–1970

CONTENTS

CONTENTS

Preface

THIS monograph deals with the question of how young precocial birds come to recognize or identify members of their
own species during the course of ontogeny. Whereas much
of the research on imprinting begins at hatching and pro-
ceeds to later stages of development (Bateson 1966, Sluckin
1965, Smith 1969), the present investigative effort begins at
hatching and recedes to embryogeny. If I had found what
I expected to find when the work began, I, too, would have
directed my experimental efforts to later rather than earlier
stages of development. I had expected to find that species
identification in birds is dependent on exposure to fellow
members of the species (conspecifics) shortly after hatching.
The corollary to this expectation was that withholding contact with conspecifics and replacing that contact with members of other species would result in a failure of the bird to
respond selectively to conspecifics and its adoption of the
substitute species. As long as I used auditory and visual
stimuli which were not representative of the species being
tested, my preconception was confirmed. However, once I

began to use species-specific auditory and visual stimuli, it became apparent that the hatchlings were selectively tuned to such stimuli, and this eventuality markedly changed my conception of the problem. The question became: How do these animals become selectively responsive to members of their own species during the course of ontogeny? Since we were dealing with newly hatched birds, an investigation of the prenatal sensory environment suggested itself. This kind of investigation has proven fascinating to me and my co-workers, and I can only hope the reader will also find the work of more than routine interest.

When one gets into a moderately complete analysis of the ontogeny of instinctive behavior, it becomes perfectly understandable why such a pursuit has failed to attract many investigators — it is very tedious work, it takes a long time to complete, and one must continually suspend judgment about the outcome lest a premature conclusion be reached. The present line of investigation has been sustained and goaded by the hope that a more unifying conception of behavioral development than those presently available may emerge from the travail. While we may be somewhat closer to that goal now, the conceptual and empirical aspects are far from complete — much more research and reflection are still required to solve the riddle of behavioral development, especially the development of adaptive or species-specific behavior. In that connection, the present work merely represents an interim progress report.

I owe a great deal to the people who assisted me with these experiments over the past six years. Due to the nature of the work, irregular and long hours were required. An unremitting regimen of week-end and night work calls for a special sense of involvement, and I am pleased to acknowledge the excellent assistance of the following persons: Anne W. Smith, Adrain Fountain, Jo Ann Winfree, Carole S. Ripley, Evelyn Strickland, Patricia B. Willis, James O'Neal, and Kenneth Ripley. Miss Winfree played an especially important role in the postnatal testing, and Mrs. Ripley's help made possible the developmental analysis of auditory perception in embryos.

Financial support came from the Research Division of the North Carolina Department of Mental Health and the National Institute of Child Health and Human Development (Research Grant HD–00878).

Development of Species Identification in Birds

1

Issues in the Development of Behavior

HISTORICALLY, the main issues in the development of behavior have revolved around the question of whether certain features of behavior are innate or whether they are acquired through experience. While most modern investigators eschew the simplistic categorization of behavior into dualistic components such as heredity-environment, innate-acquired, or instinct-learning, the conceptual problem has not been resolved. For example, when an investigator discovers that a newborn animal exhibits some behavior which (*a*) it had no opportunity to learn or practice and (*b*) the behavior appears to be adapted to the survival of the individual, it is usual to conclude that the behavior is innate or instinctive. (In many cases, *b* is not obvious, but it is "read-into" the behavior simply because the behavior itself cannot be attributed to learning or practice.)

While the terms innate or instinctive are used to describe behavior, they also imply an explanation of behavior. Innate or instinctive behavior is presumed to be the result of evolutionary processes which have endowed the species with a certain genetic complement which is specific to that species. During the development of the individual the

3

genes give rise to bodily structures including the nervous system. As these bodily structures (sensory receptors, brain, neuromusculature, etc.) become mature, they allow or make the animal behave the way it does. Schematically, this epigenetic process can be pictured in a very primitive way as follows:

Genes → Structure → Maturation → Innate Behavior

The conventional alternative to this scheme can likewise be diagrammed:

Learning
Genes → Structure →   or   → Acquired Behavior
Experience

Thus depicted, the epigenetics of behavior is controlled by two processes, and the main distinguishing feature between the two is whether maturation or experience has been responsible for the behavior. Innate behavior is a consequence of maturation, and acquired behavior is a result of learning or experience.

The above models of the epigenesis of behavior suggest an obvious technique by which all behavior can be classified into the innate or acquired category — the so-called isolation technique. In the traditional use of this procedure, the newborn animal is reared in isolation from certain stimulus objects or prohibited from practicing certain movements, and then later tested to determine its response to certain stimuli or its ability to perform certain species-typical movements. In the event that the isolated animal responds to the stimuli in an adaptive manner like other (nonisolated) members of its species, or is able to perform the species-typical motor movement like other members of its species, the behavior is classified as innate and believed to be derived from strictly maturational events which are under genetic control. Should the isolated animal not perform appropriately, the species-typical behavior of the nonisolated animals is explained on the basis of learning or experiential events which are under environmental control. While the logic of such an approach for the categorization of behavior is faultless, this approach does not come to grips with the mechanics of the development of behavior. There is certainly the illusion of having come to grips with the mechanisms of development, but this remains illusory insofar as there is no active investigation of either the structure-maturation process or the learning-experiential process; an understanding of the development of behavior requires an exact description of the specific events of development which lead to a given behavior, whether they be genetic, learning, maturational, or other kinds of events.

In recent years a number of scientists have pointed out that the urge to classify behavior as innate or acquired has involved the confusion of labeling with explaining, and that the classification of behavior into such categories has posed a conceptual barrier to further developmental investigation (e.g., Beach 1955, Kuo 1967, Lehrman 1953, Schneirla 1966, Weiss 1955). Further, the empirical research of Kuo (summarized in Kuo 1967) has led him and others even to question the validity of the innate-acquired categories: when the actual behavior of animals is observed beginning at the proper starting point for developmental study (before birth or hatching), it does not seem either useful or valid to make a distinction between the innate and acquired components.

Modern Conceptions of Development

While it may be meaningless or fruitless to attempt to understand the developmental mechanics of behavior by categorizing the end product on the basis of the isolation technique, one version or another of the technique itself is still used, and some implicit categorizations are still being made. From the writings of persons who have concerned themselves with the development of behavior, it is possible to discern two main points of view on the mechanisms of behavioral development. While the traditional dualism is still present, the modern formulation of the problem is different; research and theory are now directed squarely on the mechanisms, and these are no longer deduced solely from the end product of development. In modern dress the two traditional formulations can be pictured like this:

PREDETERMINED EPIGENESIS OF BEHAVIOR:

Genes → Structural Maturation → Function → Behavior

PROBABILISTIC EPIGENESIS OF BEHAVIOR:

Genes → Structural Maturation ⟷ Function ⟷ Behavior

Since the genetic events which give rise to structural maturation are in the domain of molecular biology and very little is yet known directly about the genetic processes which participate in neural maturation, neither formulation can or does make any specific statement about the role which genes play in behaviorial development, other than acknowledging that the genetic complement sets (unknown or unspecified) limits on such development and the presence of certain genetic combinations (e.g., those common to a species) substantially increases the probability that certain events will occur later in development. The mechanisms which bear immediate and observable relationships to behavioral development concern neural maturation and function, and it is in the conceptualization of these relationships that the two viewpoints differ. Before describing the nature and significance of this conceptual difference, it is necessary first to define the key terms in the above diagram. Neuromotor and neurosensory maturation involves four distinct but overlapping cellular processes: proliferation, migration, differentiation, and growth. At the cellular level, function refers to the electrical activity of neural cells and, at the organismic level, function refers to the overt motility of the organism. Behavior refers to activities of the animal in relation to its internal and external sensory environment. A distinction must be made between motility and behavior because it has been demonstrated that early in embryonic development certain species are capable of spontaneous motility or movement in the absence of sensory stimulation (Corner 1964, Hamburger, Wenger, and Oppenheim 1966). The purpose of the rather unorthodox inclusion of motility under "function" is to call attention to the unanswered (and previously unasked) question of whether spontaneous motility has developmental consequences for structural maturation and behavior.

While there can be little doubt that intrinsic molecular and other biochemical processes provide an indispensable impetus for the early maturation of the nervous system (i.e., during the initial proliferation and major migration period), the question is whether function and sensory stimulation play a regulative role later in maturation when the cells are still undergoing differentiation, growth, and minor shifts in terminal position. The question hinges on the influence or noninfluence of function and behavior on the maturation process. According to the predetermined epigenesis of behavior, maturation gives rise to function and behavior in a unidirectional (nonreciprocal) fashion, whereas the probabilistic viewpoint holds that there are bidirectional relationships between maturation, function, and behavior. (In the diagram, the former relationship is designated by single-headed arrows, and the latter relationship is represented by double-headed arrows.) In other words, predeterminism views the maturational process as relatively encapsulated such that it is unaffected either by function or by behavior, while probabilism assumes that maturation is affected both by function and by behavior. In more concrete terms, the main issue is whether normally occurring motor movement and sensory stimulation play a regulative role in the development of behavior, or whether behavioral development is a result of an invariant maturational sequence independent of prior motor movements and sensory stimulation. Thus, according to the view that behavioral development is predetermined by encapsulated neurosensory and neuromotor processes, withholding (or augmenting) normally occurring sensory stimulation or depriving the animal of opportunities for normal movement will have no effect on the threshold, timing, and ultimate perfection of behavior, while, according to the probabilistic view, withholding or augmenting normally occurring stimulation or muscular movement *will* affect the threshold, timing, and the ultimate perfection of behavior.

While these two views on the development of behavior usually are considered to be mutually exclusive — that is, if one is true then the other must be false — it is entirely possible that both views are correct. Certain of the very early embryonic neural and behavioral processes may be determined exclusively by molecular and other biochemical events, while later embryonic and neonatal behavior is probabilistically determined by the joint operation of molecular, biochemical, functional, and sensory stimulative events. Since it is not yet usual in developmental studies to manipulate normally occurring stimulation or motor movement prior to birth or hatching, and carefully analyze the effect of such manipulations on the threshold, timing, and perfection of later species-typical behavior, it is not possible to make an assessment of the general validity of any of these propositions. Simply stated, the current question is whether normally occurring sensory stimulation or muscular movement is essential to the normal development of behavior. The present work deals with this question as it pertains to the development of species-specific perception.

Ontogenetic Analysis of Perceptual Development
Broadly conceived, the analysis of the ontogeny of species-specific perception may be divided into three components: (*a*) an analysis of the key elements of the perceptual object (i.e., the experimental isolation of those features of the

stimulus object which are necessary to evoke a discriminative response); (*b*) an analysis of the neurophysiological and/or neuroanatomical units involved in such perception (i.e., the identification of the peripheral and central neural components of the "filtering process"); and (*c*) a macroscopic analysis of the ontogenetic events which give rise to an organism's capability to perceive in a selective manner (i.e., the effect of normally occurring stimulation on selective perception). The present work concerns (*a*) and (*c*), with emphasis on the macroscopic features of the development of species-specific perception; specifically, the relative influence of auditory and visual stimulation on the selective perception of their own species by young birds, and how the prenatal sensory environment influences such perception

At the present time, the theoretical side of species-specific perceptual development is incredibly simple and crude, being at approximately the same stage of sophistication as was the problem of cell-differentiation in the early 1900s. That stage of sophistication is admirably summarized in a quotation from W. D. Brooks (1902, pp. 490–91):

> A thoughtful and distinguished naturalist tells us that while the differentiation of the cells which arise from the egg is sometimes inherent in the egg, and sometimes induced by the conditions of development, it is more commonly mixed; but may It not be the mind of the embryologist, and not the natural world, that is mixed? Science does not deal in compromises, but in discoveries. When we say the development of the egg is inherent, must we not also say what are the relations with reference to which it is inherent? When we say it is induced, must we not also say what are the relations with reference to which it is induced? Is there any way to find this out except scientific discovery?

In the present work, in order to set the stage for "scientific discovery," it was first necessary to experimentally delineate the contribution of the auditory and visual perceptual systems to the problem of species identification in birds. While unraveling this aspect of the problem, we have employed several different species to get some idea of the interspecific generality of our conclusions. Specifically, we have used precocial forms which differed in their degree of domestication and in their nest-site ecology (hole-nesting and ground-nesting species of duck). Thus, in chapters 3 through 7, the contribution of the auditory and visual systems to species-specific perception in avian neonates is analyzed and inter-specific similarities and differences in such perception are determined. With this information in hand, the analysis is pursued to the embryonic stage of development (chapter 8) in order to determine the lower age limit of species-specific perception under conditions of normally occurring stimulation. In chapter 9, the first attempt to manipulate the normal sensory environment is made in an effort to determine if departures from the usual amount of sensory stimulation in any way alters the typical development of the embryo's responsiveness to species-specific stimulation. Finally, in chapter 10, the most significant manipulations are undertaken, those with the aim of determining the effects of prenatal and postnatal sensory deprivation on postnatal perception.

Thus, the final experiments are addressed to the rather simple question of whether normally occurring stimulation plays any role whatsoever in the ontogeny of species-specific perception. We are not asking here whether species identification is "learned" in the egg — it is too premature for us to ask that question. Our empirical understanding of the problem has only barely progressed to the point where we can ask what, if anything, could or need be learned by the embryo. Further, the answer to that question awaits the experimental isolation of the key features of the perceptual pattern; with that information in hand one can proceed knowledgeably to further analyses of the earlier stages of embryonic development to determine the influence (if any) of these early stages on later stages of perceptual development. In chapter 10 this problem is discussed, but only in a very preliminary way.

Our two main guiding ideas have been thus made explicit: (a) a complete understanding of the ontogeny of adaptive perception in neonates requires prenatal analysis and (b) the possibility that normally occurring embryonic sensory stimulation plays some role in the ontogeny of species-specific perception must be actively considered. In connection with these ideas, it should be pointed out that all of the sensory systems of the avian embryo are functional before hatching (Gottlieb 1968b). Consequently, there is some empirical basis for probing the embryological sensory environment in an analysis of the ontogeny of perception — the outcome of such probes can only be instructive. (While we have here emphasized the ontogeny of species-specific perception, the prenatal ontogeny of species-typical action patterns also lends itself to such an analysis).

To those familiar with the history of the field, it will be obvious that the present orientation to the problem of behavior owes a strong intellectual debt to the writings of W. Preyer (1885), H. C. Tracy (1926), L. Carmichael (1927), G. E. Coghill (1929), E. B. Holt (1931), D. S. Lehrman (1953), P. Weiss (1955), R. W. Sperry (1965), T. C. Schneirla (1966), and Z-Y. Kuo (1967) in particular. While the proposals of these writers differ in very significant ways, they all have been unanimous in emphasizing the necessity of studying prenatal ontogeny for a thorough understanding of the roots of postnatal behavior. With the present set of experiments, we do not anticipate being able to support or refute any detailed proposals on the ontogeny of perception (e.g., Schneirla 1965). Rather, it is hoped simply to empirically justify or validate the present orientation to the problem and to provide a firm basis for further, more detailed analyses. The previous research on the interrelationships between prenatal and postnatal behavior has dealt primarily with reflexive behavior or motor processes; the present work is of some special interest because it concerns the sensory and perceptual side of species-typical behavior.

Natural History of the Problem

As far as is known, all precocial forms of birds (waterfowl, quail, turkeys, etc.) leave the nest within a few hours or a few days after hatching. While there are inter-specific differences in the location of the nest-site, the length of stay in the nest, and the degree of precocity of the young, the generalized picture of the departure from the nest appears to be the same for most if not all of these species. Namely, as has been observed in waterfowl (Gottlieb 1965b), the hen walks (ground-nesting species) or leaps (hole-nesting species) from the nest, utters a species-characteristic call, and the young promptly leave the nest to join her. The hen continues to utter the call as she leads the young away from the nest-site. Prior to the exodus from the nest, the maternal-young bond is established and maintained by increasingly frequent vocal interchanges between the hen and her brood. The hen consistently utters the same attraction call[1] during the brooding period as she does upon the exodus. (The hen may sometimes leave the nest for short intervals during the brooding period without the young attempting to follow her [Collias and Collias 1956, Gottlieb 1963a] — in such instances, the hen does not utter the characteristic attraction call.) Thus, during the nest-departure proper, the young of ground-nesting species are exposed to both the visual and

1. The term "attraction call" is used to call attention to the functional aspect — when the call is uttered the young will climb, walk, swim, run, or jump to approach the source of the call, whether it be a tape recorder or a live hen. Thus, the specific means of ambulation is variable, and the end result is more or less invariable. In my observation of wood ducks in the postbreeding season, I have seen and heard adult hens utter this same call and thereby attract an adult drake, presumably the mate, to their side (and a source of food). Thus, the attractivness of the call would seem to persist during the lifetime of the birds, and the utterance of the call by the hen is not restricted to the maternal-young relationship.

auditory characteristics of the parent, and in hole-nesting species the young are initially exposed only to the auditory component (i.e., until the young climb out of the nest they can not see the hen). The nest-departure in ground-nesting and hole-nesting species of duck is shown in figure 1.

In a previous report on the behavior of wild ducklings in nature (Gottlieb 1963a), I mistakenly assumed that the young became "imprinted" to the maternal call during the period in the nest, by which I meant that the young could not identify a hen of their own species without prior exposure to the call. The incorrectness of this assumption was shown in later experiments (1965a), in which incubator-hatched ducklings and chicks proved to be quite responsive to the maternal call of their own species in advance of prior exposure to it. There are individual peculiarities in the call of hens of the same species; so, based on the exposure of the young to the call of their hen around the time of hatching in nature, these differences could provide the basis for subsequent individual recognition. The recent work by Tschanz (1968) with guillemots (*Uria aalge*) definitely supports such a conclusion. He has shown that exposure of hatching guillemots to calls of an individual parent establishes a preference for that call in a subsequent postnatal choice test. Given that nonexposed birds would not show such a preference, the preference of the exposed birds is obviously based on some kind of learning. In the present work, however, we are concerned with the sensory and perceptual biases of young birds and embryos in advance of exposure to species-typical maternal stimulation.

P-1   P-3

P-2   P-4

FIG. 1. Nest-departure in ground-nesting and hole-nesting species of duck.

In the exodus of the ground-nesting peking duck (*P-1* through *P-4*), a domestic form of the mallard duck, the ducklings can barely be seen until the actual departure (*P-3* and *P-4*). The microphone is attached to a parabolic reflector (background *P-3*) which helps to amplify the vocalizations of the ducklings and the hen. The reflector is installed within the first few weeks of incubation and the hens appear to accustom themselves to its presence.

14

M-1

M-2

M-3

The exodus of the ground-nesting mallard duck is shown in *M-1* through *M-3*. These semi-wild, free-wing birds sometimes use these artificial nestboxes at the Dorothea Dix Animal Behavior Field Station; otherwise, their nests are difficult to locate. A duckling can be seen in *M-1*, shortly before the hen steps out of the box. The vocalization which the hens utter when they call the young out of the nest is the same vocalization uttered during the early post-hatching period in the nest. Along with other stimulation (tactile, thermal) provided by the hen, the vocalization would appear to give her control over the behavior of the young (e.g., keeping them in the nest or encouraging them to leave the nest). In ground-nesting species the young can see and hear the parent during the exodus from the nest; the departure from the nest takes place 1 to 2 days after the young have hatched.

WD-1

WD-2

WD-3

WD-4

WD-5

WD-6

The rather dramatic exodus of the hole-nesting wood duck is shown in *WD-1* through *WD-12*. These ducks readily use artificial nestboxes, and this has played an important role in their conservation in the United States. During the late stages of incubation, some hens will stay on the nest when the lid has been removed to inspect its contents (*WD-1*); earlier in incubation the hens are much more likely to leave the nest during an inspection, and they return only after the interloper has receded from view. To get the picture in *WD-2*, the hen was deliberately flushed. The young hatch over a rather protracted period (as much as 18 hours in some cases). Just prior to the exodus, 1 to 2 days after the young have hatched, the hen appears at the exit and makes a reconnaissance (*WD-3* through *WD-6*) of the

16

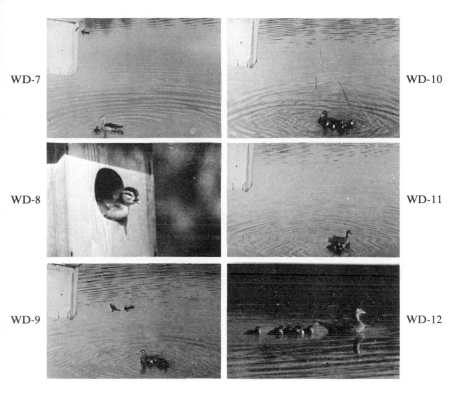

WD-7

WD-8

WD-9

WD-10

WD-11

WD-12

area before dropping below the nestbox (*WD-7*) and calling the young out of the nest. As with the mallard, the call which the wood duck hen utters at the exodus is the same call uttered throughout the posthatching period inside the box. In response to her call, the young climb up the wall inside the box, pause momentarily at the exit (*WD-7* and *WD-8*), and then leap to the water below (*WD-9*). Within 4 minutes all the ducklings are out of the nestbox (*WD-10* and *WD-11*). The hen stays in the vicinity of the nestbox until no further sounds emanate from the nestbox — the ducklings are very vocal during the exodus — and then she leads her brood to an area of thick cover in a nearby swamp. (Photos by Gus Martin and the author.)

17

2

Methodological Details of Postnatal Experiments

FOR convenience of presentation, the routine procedures for all of the postnatal experiments are described in this chapter. Since all of the experiments are interrelated, this manner of presentation reduces the repetition of details common to each of the experiments. Departures from these procedures are mentioned later in connection with the presentation of the results of experiments which involved greater or lesser sensory deprivation. The procedures for the prenatal experiments are presented in chapter 8 in connection with the findings on auditory perception prior to hatching.

Subjects
The experiments utilized one or more of four groups of birds depending on their purpose: domestic white rock chicks, domestic peking ducklings, semi-wild mallard ducklings, and wild wood ducklings.

White Rock Chicks
Unincubated white rock (*Gallus gallus*) chick eggs were delivered weekly to the laboratory by Pilch Hatcheries, Smithfield, North Carolina. Over a seven-year period the

eggs came from a number of different flocks under the control of the hatchery. The laboratory was notified each time the flock was switched, in the event that hatchability of the eggs might change, or that we might fail to repeat previous findings obtained from eggs of a different flock. The Pilch Hatchery made weekly reports to us of their hatching success from eggs of the same flock so a comparison of hatchability success could be made. This was particularly useful in two respects. Our preincubation treatment of the eggs (specified below) differed from the commercial hatchery, and we routinely came to expect that our hatchability success should run 10–20% less than Pilch's. If it was more than this amount, either the source of trouble in the laboratory was determined or the flock was changed. In addition, there were seasonal fluctuations in fertility, peaks of embryonic mortality during certain stages of incubation, and hatchability. As long as the fluctuations in the laboratory correlated with those in the commercial hatchery, no remedial action was necessary (e.g., disinfecting the incubators).

As a safeguard against introducing extraneous variability or unreliability into the results of the behavioral experiments, no birds were used from groups (usual size, 20–40 eggs) in which hatchability was less than 50% (including infertile eggs). Gunther (1965) has shown that certain behavioral changes are correlated with low hatchability, which, in his case, was produced by nonoptimal incubation temperature. Typically, hatchability ranged from 65% to 80% for the chicks in the present experiments, depending on the season of year (it was lowest during the coldest and warmest months). For reasons that have not been determined by poultry scientists, during the hatching process some chicks pip at the small end of the egg. Again, to reduce possible sources of variability or unreliability in the findings of the experiments, no chicks were used in the experiments which had hatched in this abnormal fashion. For the last three years of the chick experiments (1964–67), the hatchery delivered about 3,000 chicken eggs to the laboratory each year for use in the experiments. Due to their long-term unreliability, however, many of our experiments with chicks are not included in the present report. We are at a loss to account for the unreliability of many different kinds of results obtained with domestic chicks under the present highly controlled conditions. Our experience of seven years work with domestic chicks prompts us to urge other researchers to be cautious about using chicks for behavioral experiments.

Peking Ducklings

These ducklings (*Anas platyrhynchos*) are a domestic form of mallard (*Anas platyrhynchos*). Unincubated peking duck eggs were delivered weekly by air mail from the C. & R. Duck Farm, Westhampton, Long Island, New York. With the cooperation of the C. & R. hatchery, it was possible to take the same precautions with the hatchability of these eggs as described above with the chicken eggs. The size of the duck egg shipment varied from 60 to 200 per week from 1961–67, with an average of about 2,000 duck eggs for each of the last three years. The seasonal pattern of fertility and hatchability in the duck eggs closely paralleled the pattern with the chicken eggs.

Since the number of domestic chicken and duck eggs involved was indeed astronomical, it may be well to point out that it was rare to hatch more than 80% of the eggs for prolonged periods and that a large number of subjects was required to carry out pilot work, as well as replications of the postnatal and prenatal experiments. With regard to the matter of replication, the domestic peking duck has proven to be extremely reliable, even when the source of the eggs has been changed. For the last year (1968–69), we have been receiving peking duck eggs from a farm in Ohio, and we have had an opportunity to repeat certain of our most important experiments with these birds.

METHODOLOGY OF POSTNATAL EXPERIMENTS

Mallard Ducklings

Unincubated mallard eggs were obtained from five sources during the spring of each year. The main source was the Dorothea Dix Animal Behavior Field Station located in Raleigh, North Carolina, which was under the control of the Psychology Laboratory at Dorothea Dix Hospital. The original stock of wild mallards for the field station was obtained in 1961 from the Delta Waterfowl Research Station in Manitoba, Canada. About 40 to 80 free-wing mallards have been maintained at the station since that time. In 1961 and 1962, semi-wild mallard eggs were also purchased from a private supplier, John Whalen in Bath, North Carolina. In 1966 and 1967, eggs were obtained from two game farms in Minnesota and the U. S. Fish and Wildlife Service, Patuxent Wildlife Research Center, Laurel, Maryland, through the courtesy of James McGilvrey.

Except at the beginning and end of each season, hatchability of the mallard eggs was usually quite high (80%). When less than 50% of a group or clutch hatched, the hatchlings were not used in the experiments. In the rare case when a mallard pipped at the small end of the egg during hatching, it was not used in the experiments.

Considering the diversity of sources of the mallard eggs, it was particularly important to replicate the main behavioral findings from one year to the next with eggs from the same source or during the same year with eggs from different sources. Unless noted to the contrary, only those findings which have been replicated are reported in this monograph.

Wood Ducklings

Wood duck (*Aix sponsa*) eggs were collected each season at the Dorothea Dix Animal Behavior Field Station and a private waterfowl reserve in Raleigh, North Carolina. During the period covered by the experiments reported here, there were 42 artificial wood duck nesting boxes at the Dorothea

Dix Field Station and 11 such boxes at the private reserve, yielding about 300 eggs each season. These cypress boxes are of a type widely employed throughout the United States by wildlife management specialists who study wood duck nesting ecology. Pictures of the nest boxes are shown in figure 1, chapter 1.

For the collection of wood duck eggs, each nest box at the two locations was checked periodically to determine if it was in use and, if so, the stage of laying or incubation of the eggs. From 1961 to 1963, the unincubated eggs were collected as soon as they were discovered. In those years, hatchability was quite low (60% or less). In subsequent years, with few exceptions, the wood duck eggs were collected after the hen had incubated them for one to three weeks. Hatchability in the laboratory then rose to 80% or better. Since the incubation period of wood duck eggs is 30 to 35 days in nature, and the hen does not begin calling to the eggs until very late in incubation, it seemed safe to allow the eggs to begin incubation in the field. The same precautions regarding hatchability and replicability of behavioral results mentioned in the above section on mallard eggs were taken with wood duck eggs. There has been a great deal of variability in certain findings with the wood ducklings (particularly on selectivity of auditory response to wood duck and other maternal calls) from year to year and from clutch to clutch in the same year, so, for this reason, we have not been able to place great confidence in the results on this particular point. Otherwise, it has been possible to obtain consistent results with the wood ducks. It may very well be that uniform results on the selective nature of the wood duckling's auditory response can only be obtained if the eggs are incubated from the beginning in the laboratory (i.e., under standard conditions in sound-shielded rooms and incubators). On the other hand, we are at a loss to explain the clutch-to-clutch variability in eggs that were so incubated.

METHODOLOGY OF POSTNATAL EXPERIMENTS

Other Species

Although there is a temptation to mention preliminary and incomplete work with other species in a monograph of original experiments, that temptation has been resisted since the results of preliminary or incomplete experiments, though interesting, may well lead to erroneous conclusions. We (my co-workers and I) have been interested in trying to extend our comparative work in several directions. For example, it would be of interest and importance to compare the selective perception of species in wild chickens (jungle fowl) to that of domestic ones; to see how geese compare to ducks; to determine how other hole-nesters compare to the wood ducklings; and how monomorphic ground-nesters might compare to the dimorphic, ground-nesting mallard. At the present writing these are all either unstarted or unfinished problems and are likely to remain that way as we turn our attention almost exclusively to the embryological roots of perception.

Refrigeration

Although there has been no attempt in the present work to delineate very exact "critical periods," but only to grossly bracket the age periods involved, we have continued to use one or another refrigeration technique prior to incubation to allow the developmental age of the animals to be calculated, as well as using the more routine convention of specifying posthatch age in the postnatal experiments.

Prior to incubation, the white rock chick eggs and the peking duck eggs were placed in refrigerators. The chick eggs were refrigerated at $37° \pm 2°F.$ for 6 days and duck eggs at $29° \pm 1°F.$ for 3 days. After being removed from the refrigerators, the eggs were held at room temperature ($68°$–$72°F.$) for 5 to 6 hours and then placed in incubators. This procedure kills any embryos that may have been somewhat advanced in development at the time of laying (Gottlieb 1963b). Therefore, the developmental age of the embryos or hatchlings which were unaffected by the treatment could be calculated with somewhat greater accuracy.

The unincubated mallard and wood duck eggs were held at optimum storage temperature (55°F.) for 1 to 7 days prior to incubation. Wood duck eggs which were known to be partially incubated were not submitted to refrigeration, but were placed in an incubator within 45 minutes after they were collected in the field. The eggs were kept warm (80°– 90°F.) in transit from the field.

Incubation

A great deal of care was taken to control sensory stimulation and to regulate other conditions during the incubation of all eggs. The four air-conditioned rooms housing seven incubators were individually sound-shielded, and their temperature was thermostatically regulated at all times of the year. The doors to the incubator rooms were opened only during periods of silence in the laboratory, and no conversation (other than limited whispering) occurred in these rooms. In addition to exchanging and moving the air, the air conditioners and the incubator fans provided a fairly constant level of background noise (73–75 dB SPL) inside the incubators. Each species of egg was incubated in a different room, so it was not possible for different species to stimulate each other.

All eggs were incubated in electric forced-draft machines at a temperature of 99° to 101°F., with an average around 99¾ °F. The relative humidity was between 55% to 65% for chick eggs and 60% to 70% for duck eggs. All eggs were incubated with the long axis of the egg parallel to the ground. The eggs were turned either 8 times daily automatically or 4 times daily by hand. At one time or another all of the species experienced both turning regimens.

The general procedure of incubation was the same for all species; the details differed only according to the length of incubation of the species concerned. Where length of incubation is calculated in terms of number of days completed, white rock chicks usually hatch on Day 20 (i.e., during the 21st day of incubation), peking ducks hatch on Day 26 or Day 27, mallard ducks hatch about Day 25, and wood ducks hatch on Day 29 to 31 if they are incubated from start to finish in the laboratory. As is the usual hatchery practice, the eggs were transferred to a hatching tray, that is, they were no longer turned during the last 10% to 15% of the incubation period. This was late on Day 17 or early on Day 18 for chick eggs, late Day 23 or early Day 24 for peking eggs, Day 22 for mallard eggs, and Day 26 for wood duck eggs.

Although the incubators were otherwise unlighted, they were lighted for brief periods when the progress of the hatch was being checked. (The incubator rooms were illuminated by "black" light.) The hatch was checked frequently and the overall period of illumination was short (1–2 mins.). Most of the birds were removed well within 3 hours after they had hatched, though some of them remained in the unlighted hatching tray for as long as 4 hours when the hatch was sparse and the checks less frequent. When a bird was removed from the hatching tray, it was placed in a small carton which had small pin holes in the sides and top to admit heated air. Each carton had a slip of paper on it identifying the bird according to its group, when it had started incubation, and when it had hatched. The carton with the bird inside was then transferred to a brooder housing other birds from the same group.

As far as auditory and visual stimulation is concerned, the usual incubation procedure (above) and brooding procedure (below) allowed the bird very little light stimulation and some auditory stimulation. To the extent that the hatchlings' vocalizations penetrated the background noise level of the incubator and room air-conditioner, the hatchlings could hear themselves and their sibs. There was also a limited opportunity for them to see themselves when the light was turned on to check the hatch. Other than the noise from the air conditioner, the incubator fan (motor), and possibly the opening and closing of the incubator door, that was the extent of the possibilities for visual and auditory experience under the usual conditions of incubation. More deprived and enhanced conditions of stimulation during incubation or brooding are described later in connection with the experiments which were specifically addressed to assessing the influence of increased sensory deprivation or specific forms of sensory augmentation.

Brooding

Each bird resided in an individual carton (approximately a 4-inch cube) in the brooder. As with incubation, each species was segregated in a separate sound-shielded room during brooding. Temperature in the brooders ranged from 86° to 92°F. The heat was provided by thermostatically controlled brooder lamps from overhead. Room air-conditioners provided a background noise level of 68 to 71 dB SPL inside the brooders. To the extent that the hatchlings' vocalizations penetrated the background noise level, the birds could hear themselves and their sibs. To a very limited degree, the birds also had an opportunity to see parts of their own bodies from the brooder light which leaked through the air holes in the sides and tops of their cartons.

Since all of the birds were tested before they were 50 hours old, neither food nor water was made available to the birds at any time. Marcström (1960) has shown that capercaillie chicks (*Tetrao urogallus*) have an adequate store of food from their yolk sac for at least 46 hours after hatching, and Kear (1965) and Marcström (1966) have verified this result with mallard ducklings. In nature, ducklings are not fed in the nest, and they do not usually leave the nest until the second day after hatching.

Test Apparatus

The circular apparatus, shown in figure 2, was a modification of the one designed by Ramsay and Hess (1954; Hess,

FIG. 2. Postnatal test console and apparatus. From the console, the observer can view the duckling through a mirror (upper right) suspended over the test apparatus. The test apparatus is completely enclosed by a black curtain. Foot-pedals below the console actuate the time clocks for recording latency and duration of approach or following.

1958). The floor and walls were painted flat black, and the curtain enclosing the apparatus was also black. The temperature at the floor of the apparatus was maintained at 72° to 78°F. The birds were observed through a mirror which hung above the apparatus. Radial white stripes (½ inch wide) were painted at 12-inch intervals on the floor so the observer could accurately gauge whether the bird was meeting the criteria for a following-response (specified below). Likewise, partial ellipses were painted on the floor of the apparatus so the birds' approach-response to stationary stimulus objects could be objectively scored (described below).

Each stimulus object was equipped internally with a volumetric 4-inch permanent magnet speaker with a frequency range of 35 to 16,000 Hz. The speakers were mounted on the underside of the stimulus objects and faced the floor. The stimulus objects were suspended from either arm of a т-shaped pole which rose from the center of the floor of the circular apparatus. In this connection, there were two important differences between the present apparatus and the one used by Ramsay and Hess (1954) and Hess (1958, 1959). First, the open field design of the present apparatus allowed the bird to see and approach the stimulus objects from any point in the apparatus. Since the Ramsay and Hess apparatus employed a circular runway walled on both sides, their birds could only see the object when it was nearby. A significant difference between the two apparatuses was in the procedure in exposing the birds to the moving objects. In the present case, 10 to 15 seconds after the bird was placed at the starting point in the apparatus, the stimulus object automatically began to move, and it continued to move in one direction on a circular path around the apparatus regardless of the bird's behavior. In contrast, it was the procedure of Ramsay and Hess (oral communication, 1958) to back up the model and move it away from the bird a number of times if the bird was not immediately responsive to it. This procedure was required partly because of the design of the Ramsay-Hess apparatus (i.e., if the bird did not follow, the object disappeared from the bird's view around the bend of the circular runway); therefore it was expeditious for Ramsay and Hess to reverse the direction of the model rather than let it run its course. While this procedure has its merits, especially in inducing otherwise recalcitrant birds to follow the object, it has the drawback that each bird is treated somewhat differently and these differences may affect one's results in subtle or unknown ways. Consequently, it was to avoid this problem that the present apparatus consisted of an open-field design and an invariant routine of presenting the stimulus objects to each bird.

The presentation procedure went as follows. Ten to 15 seconds after the bird was placed in a routine starting spot in the apparatus, the stimulus object or objects began to move around a 14-foot circular path at the rate of one revolution every 58 seconds. The total time per revolution included an automatic 5-second pause after each 20 seconds of movement. The exact starting position of the stimulus object(s) in relation to the bird differed according to the various conditions of testing, and these conditions are specified in connection with each experiment.

Stimulus Objects
The main visual stimulus objects used singly or in combination in the experiments were stuffed hens of various species (white rock chicken, peking duck, mallard duck, wood duck) and a male mallard decoy. As mentioned above, all of these objects were equipped with internal speakers. These objects are shown in figure 3.

The main auditory stimuli used in the experiments were natural calls of hens (domestic chicken, mallard, pintail duck, wood duck, and mandarin duck) recorded in the pertinent context of the primary stage of the formation of the mother-young bond in the field. These particular vocalizations have been variously labeled attraction calls, leading calls, and exodus calls — all are referred to here as maternal attraction calls. With the exception of the chicken and pintail maternal attraction calls, all of the calls were recorded by the author in the field immediately prior to or during the exodus of the brood from the nest. These calls were the ones uttered by the hen in stimulating the young to follow her departure from the nest under undisturbed conditions, that is, they were not fear, warning, or alarm calls such as the hen utters when she is disturbed by a predator or a person near her nest. These latter calls usually precede the

Fig. 3. Visual stimulus objects. From left to right, peking duck, mallard duck, mallard drake, wood duck hen, and white rock chicken hen. Each object is fitted with a speaker in its underside. During the experiments, the objects are suspended from either end of the center pole by means of a chain. A receptacle for a speaker plug is mounted on the dorsal side of each object.

"broken wing" routine or the outright fleeing of the hen and the dispersal or "freezing" of the young. The maternal attraction call of the domestic chicken was originally recorded by Nicholas Collias (1960) in the context of a domestic hen leading her chicks shortly after hatching. In 1959, with the assistance of W. W. H. Gunn, Robert I. Smith recorded the pintail maternal attraction call during his extensive naturalistic study of the social behavior of pintail ducks at the Delta Waterfowl Research Station, Manitoba, Canada. Dr. Smith kindly allowed me to analyze the tape recording and make a copy of the call. It should be mentioned that in nature it would be very difficult to hear any of these calls without amplification equipment, since they are uttered at very low intensity.

For the present experimental purposes, each of the maternal calls was rerecorded such that it repeated itself at approximately 3-second intervals over an entire tape. The burst and rate characteristics of the experimental calls are shown in table 1, and a spectographic analysis is shown in figure 4. The experimental maternal calls were free of other sounds such as the cheeping of ducklings or chicks.

Two other calls were used: these were certain vocalizations made by peking ducklings and white rock chicks around the time of hatching. These neonatal or perinatal calls were obtained in the laboratory; they are difficult to characterize verbally in that they are not what are commonly considered to be distress-type peeping or contentment-like twittering, though they are more similar to the latter. These are very low intensity calls that duck and chick embryos utter before hatching when they are in the air-space of the egg, and they also emit these calls after hatching when they are in quiet, undisturbed, brooding-like situations (Gottlieb and Vandenbergh 1968). For experimental purposes these calls were rerecorded like the maternal calls, so they repeated themselves about every 3 seconds for the length of the tape. The characteristics of the peking duckling and white rock chick perinatal or neonatal vocalizations are shown in table 1 and figure 4. In figure 5 an analysis is shown of the communal brooding-like calls of 10 ducklings aged 10 to 30 hours (Day 27–28). This recording (3 minutes in length) was used in connection with the augmentation experiments described in chapter 9. The purpose of this recording was to expose the embryos to all the predominant frequencies to which they are ordinarily exposed, and to do so in a controlled fashion. Distress-type calls were omitted from the tape because they occur infrequently during normal, undisturbed incubation and brooding. The calls on the tape peak at 2,500 Hz with a small harmonic at 5,000 Hz. The various

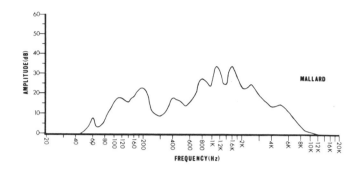

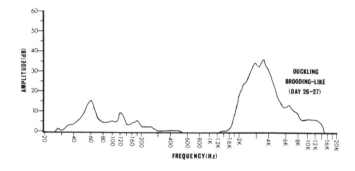

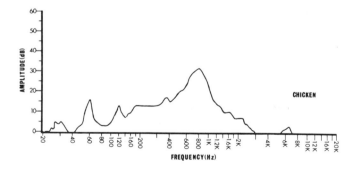

FIG. 4. Frequency analysis of the calls used in the experiments. (Low frequency noise artifacts have not been edited out; see text and table 1 for further description of each call.)

32

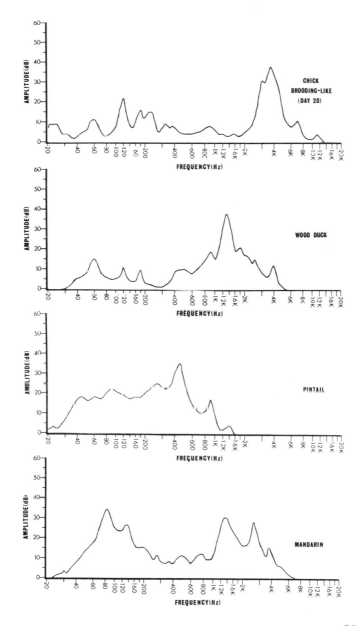

33

TABLE 1
Burst, Rate, and Fundamental Frequency Characteristics of Maternal and Perinatal Calls Used in the Present Experiments

Call	Single Burst (notes and secs.)		Average Rate (notes per sec.)	Fundamental Frequency (Hz)
Mallard ♀	9	2.2	4.1	1,125; 1,600
Duckling brooding-like (Day 26–27)	8	1.8	4.4	3,400
Chicken ♀	7	2.8	2.5	775
Chick brooding-like (Day 20)	7	1.5	4.7	3,600
Wood duck ♀	13	1.75	7.4	1,300
Pintail ♀	9	1.6	5.6	440
Mandarin ♀	9	1.0	9.0	1,325

NOTE: For experimental purposes, the same burst of any given call is repeated at approximately 3-sec. intervals for the duration of the tape. The rate of each call was determined by dividing the number of notes by the total time from the beginning of the first note to the end of the last note in the burst. Since the notes do not occur at equal intervals within the burst, the rate presented for each call is an average for the entire burst. The mandarin call has an outstanding harmonic at 2,600 Hz and a minor one at 3,900 Hz (see fig. 4). The brooding-like vocalizations are produced by highly developed embryos as well as hatchlings, beginning around Day 24–25 in duck embryos and late on Day 19 in chick embryos. The fundamental frequency of these vocalizations changes with age (Gottlieb and Vandenbergh 1968). The information presented in this table is intended as a partial descriptive analysis of the calls; the extent to which rate and frequency are important to the birds is discussed in chapter 10.

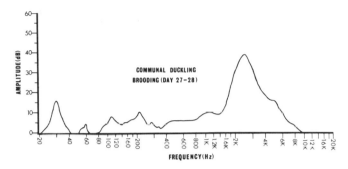

FIG. 5. Frequency analysis of 3-minute segment of brooding-like calls obtained from 10 communally brooded ducklings less than 30 hours old. This call was used in the augmentation experiments in chapter 9.

calls which embryos emit have been described and depicted by Gottlieb and Vandenbergh (1968, pp. 310–14).

The maternal and perinatal calls (figs. 4 and 5) were analyzed by a Brüel and Kjaer Type 2107 Frequency Analyzer and a B and K Type 2305 Level Recorder. When the frequency spectra were redrawn for publication, the 60-cycle noise artifacts (and harmonics thereof) were faithfully reproduced. By using a dual-beam oscilloscope (signal on one beam, analyzer on the other beam), it was possible to definitely ascertain that the peaks at 60 Hz and below were due almost entirely to noise and do not represent signal on any of the calls (there is a minor signal component at 60 Hz in the pintail and mandarin calls). Further, the 120 Hz peak represents noise on all the tapes except the mallard (substantial signal) and pintail (slight signal with predominant noise). For some unknown reason, the 85 Hz peak on the mandarin call is made up entirely of tremendous noise envelopes extending from 60 through 140 Hz; some signal (minor) is first evident on the mandarin tape at 500 Hz.

The fundamentals for all the calls listed in table 1 have been verified by the oscilloscopic method (above), and they do represent total signal. The low frequency noise problem

35

stems from the fact that some of the calls were recorded in the field using electrically powered tape recorders and, in some cases, the procedure of rerecording the calls in the laboratory has added low frequency noise artifacts, the audible portions of which are heard as low, background "static."

Over the long period covered by the present report, different tape recorders, speakers, testing rooms, and sound level meters were employed at one time or another. With respect to the dB levels of the test calls, the main emphasis was on the maintenance of a standard intensity level and, in the choice tests, equalization of the dB range of both calls. To correct for drifts in the equipment, it was necessary to check the sound level readings a number of times during each experiment; otherwise it would be possible for unrecognized biases to occur which could invalidate the results. Rather than narrate all the various dB levels yielded by the different sound-level meters under the various conditions over the seven years covered by the present report, our specific dB readings (re: 0.0002 dyne/cm^2) for the last six months should suffice for an evaluation of the procedure. At the point where the bird was placed in the apparatus, a Brüel and Kjaer Type 2203 Precision Sound Level Meter (directional microphone) set at 70 dB read as follows on Scale B (fast): mallard call, 66–72 dB; mandarin call, 70–72 dB; chicken call, 67–72 dB; wood duck call, 69–72 dB; pintail call, 60–72 dB; peking duckling call, 63–72 dB; and white rock chick, 68–72 dB. As an additional precaution in the simultaneous choice tests, to avoid possible directional biases, the position of the calls and/or visual replicas was systematically interchanged during each experiment.

Behavioral Tests
At the outset the main questions to be answered were: can a bird hatched in an incubator in the laboratory (i.e., a maternally naive bird) identify a hen of its own species? If so, what is the contribution of the maternal call and the visual

attributes of the hen? Which modality is more important and how do the two modalities interact? To answer these questions several variations of four basic perceptual test situations were employed.

Audiovisual Test

In audiovisual tests various maternal replicas emitting one or another of the maternal calls were presented to the bird. The object was either presented alone to determine its effect in eliciting the following-response or it was presented in competition with another maternal replica emitting a different call (simultaneous choice test) to determine the bird's

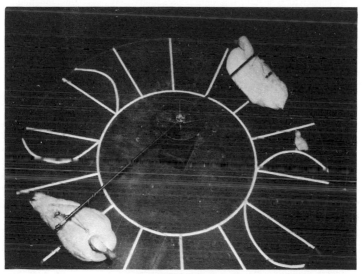

Fig. 6. Simultaneous audiovisual choice test. Two similar visual stimulus objects emit different maternal calls to determine the bird's ability to select the species-typical audiovisual configuration. In the picture above, two stuffed peking hens are moving and the bird is following the hen emitting the species-typical maternal call (mallard).

ability to select the species-typical stimulus configuration (figure 6).

TWO

Visual Test

In a visual test the bird was presented a silent visual stimulus object to determine the effectiveness of the purely visual attributes of the maternal replicas in stimulating the following-response. The purpose of this kind of test was to determine whether the visual attributes of the hen were a sufficient basis for species identification.

Auditory Test

In these tests (fig. 7) an opaque wall was interposed between the bird and a box housing a speaker. In this way it was possible to determine the effectiveness of the calls in stimu-

FIG. 7. Simultaneous auditory choice test. Two different maternal calls emanate from two sound sources which are not visible to the bird (speakers are housed in boxes suspended from each end of the center pole). In the photo above, a peking duckling is within the approach area of one of the calls during a simultaneous auditory approach test. For a test involving the following-response, the speakers move about the perimeter of the apparatus.

lating the approach- and following-response of the birds, independent of visual stimulation from the stuffed hens. In simultaneous choice tests, the birds were presented two calls emanating from two independent sources to determine the birds' auditory preference and their ability to make the appropriate discrimination based on maternal auditory stimulation alone.

Auditory vs. Visual Test

To determine whether the visual or the auditory attributes of the hen were most important or more attractive, the birds were placed in a situation (simultaneous choice test) in which they could follow either the silent stuffed hen or the maternal call emanating from a nonvisible sound source (fig. 8).

Response Measures

To determine the birds' perceptual preferences and their ability to discriminate species-typical stimuli, two behavioral measures were used — the approach-response to stationary stimuli and the following-response to moving stimuli. As a rule these two measures usually correlated very well, but the following-response proved to be the best measure in revealing the potency of a given stimulus to evoke and sustain a response.

Approach-Response

When a bird approached within 4 inches of a stationary visual stimulus source, it began accumulating a score (time in seconds) for as long as it remained within the 4-inch zone around the source. A partial ellipse designating the 4-inch zone was painted on the floor underneath the stationary stimulus object, so there was no difficulty in objectively timing an approach-response. The nearest point of the approach area from the spot where the bird was placed in the apparatus was 26 inches. For an approach test involving

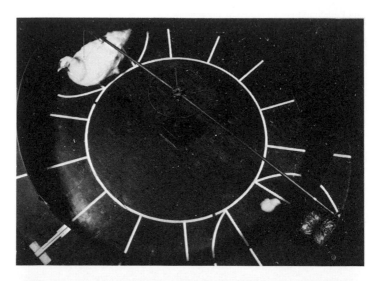

Fig. 8. Auditory vs. visual choice test. In these tests the stuffed hen moves silently about the apparatus while her call emanates from the box moving at the opposite end of the center pole. In the top photo, a chick is shown following the chicken ma-

ternal call in preference to a silent chicken hen. In the next picture, a mallard duckling is following the mallard maternal call in preference to a silent mallard hen, and in the above picture a peking duckling is following the species-specific maternal call in preference to a silent peking hen.

two sources of stimulation (simultaneous choice test) instead of only one, the stimuli and the respective approach zones were at opposite 90 degree angles to the spot where the bird was placed in the apparatus. To avoid the possibility of a directional or positional bias in the simultaneous choice tests, the position of the two stimuli was systematically exchanged prior to testing each bird. With the approach-response, as well as with the following-response, it was possible to record the latency of the response (number of seconds elapsed from the start of the test to the bird's approach within the designated area) and the duration of the response (number of seconds spent inside the approach zone).

For an auditory test involving the approach-response, a circular opaque black cloth wall was interposed between the duckling and the box housing the speaker, as shown in figure 7. In the auditory tests, the duckling was credited with an approach-response when it moved inside that portion of the elliptical approach area to which it had access.

Following-Response

For quantitative purposes as well as for the reliability of the results, it was necessary to specify artificial criteria for a following-response and to apply these criteria literally. A following score (time in seconds) was earned only if the bird was within 12 inches to the rear or 4 inches to the side of the moving visual stimulus source, with its head oriented toward and its body moving in the same direction as the source. Scoring began only after the bird had taken 3 steps under these conditions. If the bird's entire body was in front of the source, no following time was awarded. If the duckling was fulfilling the criteria for following prior to the periodic 5-second pause in the movement of the source, the bird continued to accumulate time provided it stayed within 4 inches to the side or rear of the source during the pause. If the bird had not been following the source before the pause, but ran over to the source during the pause, no credit was given until following ensued. For an auditory test involving the following-response, a wall (see fig. 7) was interposed between the duckling and the speaker. The criteria for following remained the same except that the appropriately oriented and moving duckling was credited with following when it was within 8½ inches to the side or 12 inches to the rear of the concealed sound. As can be seen in figure 7, the ducklings could approach the speaker from only one side in the auditory test, while in the audiovisual and visual tests they could follow the replica from either side (fig. 6).

Despite the restrictive nature and rigorous application of the above criteria for following, some birds achieved what appeared to be a chance following score of a few seconds during some of the longer following tests. To rule out chance scores, no bird scoring 10 seconds or less was considered to have followed the source.

The author and two assistants were responsible for carrying out the postnatal tests during the seven-year period covered by the present report. Sporadic checks on interobserver agreement, with two of the observers scoring the following-response of the same bird, showed a maximum difference of 5% between observers in timing birds which followed in the range from 40 to 300 seconds. This was considered a highly acceptable degree of reliability.

Statistics

The Chi-Square Test was used to determine the reliability of differences in the proportion of birds which approached or followed in each condition. The Mann-Whitney U-Test was applied to differences in latency and duration of approach or following (time in seconds) between each condition, and only included data from birds which had actually accumulated an approach or following score (i.e., nonresponders were excluded from these analyses). Unless otherwise specified, all p-values reported in the text are for two-tailed tests.

3

Effectiveness of Species-Specific Auditory vs. Visual Stimulation in Eliciting and Maintaining the Following-Response of Domestic Chicks and Ducklings

THE aim of the present experiment was to determine the respective potencies of maternal auditory and visual stimulation in eliciting the following-response of maternally naive chicks and ducklings. To accomplish this aim, 167 domestic white rock chicks and 93 peking ducklings were exposed to one of three 20-minute test conditions with mobile stimuli: audiovisual condition (species-specific maternal call emanating from stuffed hen); auditory condition (species-specific maternal call without hen); and visual condition (stuffed hen without maternal call). The posthatch age at testing for the chicks was 8 to 47 hours (developmental age of 20 days, 15 hours to 22 days, 10 hours) and for the ducks it was 12 to 31 hours (developmental age of 27 days, 0 hours to 28 days, 12 hours).

Results
As shown in table 2, the auditory component of the maternal parent instigated a higher proportion of following than the visual component in both species. In the ducklings, the

44

TABLE 2

Relative Effectiveness of Species-Specific Maternal Auditory and Visual Stimulation on Following-Response of Maternally Naive Chicks and Peking Ducklings during Twenty-Minute Following Test

Experimental Condition	Vocal and/or Model	N	Percentage Following	Latency (in sec.) M	S.D.	Duration (in sec.) M	S.D.
White rock chicks							
Auditory	Maternal call	25	92	200.4	228.8	173.5	108.9
Visual	Stuffed ♀ chicken	63	25	595.9	272.5	89.4	163.2
Audiovisual	Stuffed ♀ chicken and maternal call	79	72	297.4	204.6	371.0	293.8
Peking ducklings							
Auditory	Maternal call	25	52	331.9	297.1	121.9	165.1
Visual	Stuffed ♀ peking	30	7	607.0	151.3	300.5	181.7
Audiovisual	Stuffed ♀ peking and maternal call	38	92	261.3	243.6	668.7	351.2

NOTE: A higher proportion of chicks followed in the auditory condition (auditory vs. visual, $p<.001$; auditory vs. audiovisual, $p=.08$). More of the chicks followed in the audiovisual than in the visual condition ($p<.001$). The chicks which responded in the auditory and audiovisual conditions began following sooner than the responders in the visual condition ($p<.001$ and $p<.0001$, respectively). Chicks in the audiovisual condition followed more persistently than both the auditory group ($p=.01$) and the visual group ($p<.0006$). Chicks in the auditory condition followed more persistently than the visual group ($p<.001$). More of the ducklings responded in the audiovisual than in the auditory ($p<.02$) and visual conditions ($p<.002$). More of the ducklings responded in the auditory than in the visual condition ($p<.002$). Latency was shorter for the ducklings in the audiovisual than in the visual condition ($p<.06$). Ducklings followed less persistently in the auditory than in the audiovisual ($p<.0006$) and visual conditions ($p=.10$). There was no reliable difference in the ducklings' duration of following in the audiovisual and visual conditions — only 2 ducklings followed in the visual condition, whereas 35 out of 38 followed in the audiovisual condition.

$M=$ mean; S.D. $=$ standard deviation (so throughout).

45

audiovisual condition elicited a higher proportion of following than the auditory or visual conditions, but in the chicks the auditory condition tended to elicit an even higher incidence of following than the audiovisual condition ($p = .08$). The chicks responded most slowly (latency) in the visual conditions, and the ducklings showed an unreliable tendency in the same direction. In both species, the audiovisual condition maintained following (duration) better than either the auditory or visual conditions. The chicks showed more persistent following in the auditory than in the visual condition. However, the 2 ducklings which responded in the visual condition tended to follow more persistently ($p = .10$) than the 13 ducklings which responded in the auditory condition. (Only 7% of the ducklings responded in the visual condition, whereas 52% responded in the auditory condition, so the comparison of duration of following in these two conditions should be given less weight than the proportion which followed in each condition.) As is usual in such experiments, the individual variability in latency and duration of following was very high (see standard deviations in table 2).

Regarding interspecific comparisons, the chicks responded more strongly than the ducklings in the auditory condition (percent followed [$p = .006$] and duration of following [$p = .04$]). In the visual condition, a higher proportion of chicks than ducklings followed ($p = .06$), but the few ducklings which followed tended to do so more strongly ($p = .10$) than the chicks. In the audiovisual condition, more of the ducklings followed ($p = .02$), and they did so more persistently than the chicks ($p < .0001$).

For the sake of further comparison, table 3 shows the performance of wild hole-nesting wood ducklings and ground-nesting mallards under similar experimental conditions (Gottlieb 1968a). As can be seen, the wild birds showed a pattern of responsiveness which is essentially similar to the domestic birds: their response in the audiovisual condition was stronger than in either of the other conditions, and the auditory condition tended to be more potent than the visual condition.

To clarify the interpretation of the above results, one further experiment was conducted. In this experiment, the

TABLE 3

Following-Response of Wood Ducklings and Mallards to the Audiovisual, Auditory, and Visual Components of their Respective Maternal Parent during Twenty-Minute Following Test

	Audiovisual	p	Auditory	p	Visual
Wood Ducks ($N = 72$)					
Followed	84%	.07	59%	s	11%
Ave. latency (sec.)	300.7	s	78.7	s	474.5
Ave. duration (sec.)	750.8	s	79.4	ns	229.0
Mallards ($N = 60$)					
Followed	95%	s	50%	ns	30%
Ave. latency (sec.)	265.3	.07	193.5	s	561.8
Ave. duration (sec.)	440.8	s	98.5	ns	127.8

NOTE: The p-values in the table refer to data in the columns to which they are interposed. Inter-species comparisons follow. Wood ducks showed shorter latency (.06) than mallards in response to the auditory component. There were no differences between wood ducks and mallards in response to the visual component. Wood ducks showed longer duration of following than mallards to the audiovisual component.
$s = p < .05$. $ns = p > .05$.

maternal call was placed in simultaneous opposition to the silent maternal replica (auditory vs. visual choice test). Since the response of the peking ducklings was so low in the visual condition of the previous experiment, they were not tested in the present experiment. In their stead previously published data from wood ducklings and mallard ducklings (Gottlieb 1968a) are shown in table 5.

As can be seen in table 4, the white rock chicks showed an unequivocal preference for their maternal call over the visual replica of the hen in the simultaneous auditory vs.

TABLE 4
Response of Chicks in Simultaneous Choice Test between Chicken Maternal Call and Silent Maternal Replica

N	Percentage Responding	Percentage Preference		Mean Latency (sec.)		Mean Duration (sec.)	
		Call	Replica	Call	Replica	Call	Replica
		Four-Minute Approach Test					
20	70	100	0	114.4	...	93.3	...
		Ten-Minute Following Test					
20	55	91	9	160.0	473.0	40.7	11.0

NOTE: Only one chick responded to the visual replica (10-min. following test).

visual choice test. The wood ducklings and mallards demonstrated this same preference in an equally clear fashion (table 5).

TABLE 5

Response of Wood Ducklings and Mallards in Choice Test between Maternal Call and Maternal Visual Replica during Fourteen-Minute Following Test

	Maternal Call	Maternal Replica
Wood ducks ($N = 15$)		
Percent responded	53	0
Ave. latency (sec.)	73.3	. . .
Ave. duration (sec.)	35.3	. . .
Mallards ($N = 20$)		
Percent responded	45	0
Ave. latency (sec.)	87.6	. . .
Ave. duration (sec.)	66.6	. . .

NOTE: There was no difference between wood ducklings and mallards in response to their respective maternal calls.

Discussion

In answer to the main question, species-specific maternal auditory stimulation is more potent than maternal visual stimulation in all species tested (domestic white rock chicks, domestic peking ducklings, wild mallard ducklings, and wild wood ducklings). Thus, this generalization holds across species which differ in their degree of domestication as well as ecological status (hole-nesters and ground-nesters). The prepotency of maternal auditory stimulation is relative — all the duck species showed their strongest response to the combined presence of the maternal attraction call and visual replica of the parent (audiovisual condition). In this respect the chicks differed somewhat from the ducklings — a somewhat higher proportion of the chicks responded to the maternal call alone than to the audiovisual combination. However, the audiovisual combination maintained the chicks' following response at a significantly higher level than the call by itself. In general, all of the species showed their poorest or weakest response to the purely visual attributes of their parent. In the auditory vs. visual choice tests, all the species demonstrated an unequivocal preference for their maternal call. These results strongly suggest that species identification is based primarily on auditory perception in the early stages of development in the species studied. Under normal conditions in the field, of course, the parent is not only a source of auditory stimulation, but she also provides visual, tactile, and thermal stimulation. As we (Gottlieb and Simner 1969) and others have previously pointed out, however, under field conditions ducklings frequently lose sight of their parent in swamps, marshes, or other grassy terrain, so the ducklings' ability to respond to the maternal call in the absence of the hen's visual presence plays an important role in the field as well as in the laboratory.

It is of some interest that the present findings also hold for non–species-specific stimulation. In a two-phase study, Gottlieb and Simner (1969) first equated the attractiveness of flickering auditory and visual stimulation in evoking the approach-response of domestic chicks and then tested the animals with the equated auditory and visual stimuli in a simultaneous choice situation. The birds showed a preference for the auditory stimuli at both 24 and 48 hours after hatching, thereby demonstrating the behavioral prepotency of the auditory system over the visual system in the early posthatching stage of development. Other workers, using different procedures and various auditory and visual stimuli, have also found auditory stimuli to be prepotent over visual stimuli in the young of all precocial avian species tested to date (Boyd and Fabricius 1965, Fischer 1966, Porter and Stettner 1968, Ramsay 1951, Smith and Bird 1963).

The similarity in sensory preferences (auditory over visual) in all species tested may stem from a similar prenatal background. During embryological development in birds, the auditory system becomes functional before the visual system (Gottlieb 1968b). In addition, during the normal course of incubation, the birds are exposed to their own self-produced vocalizations both before and after hatching, and such exposure enhances subsequent responsiveness to the maternal call (Gottlieb 1966). On the prenatal side, decreased exposure to the vocalizations of sibs is associated with a decrease in the embryo's responsiveness to the maternal call (Gottlieb 1968b). This aspect of the problem requires still further analysis (see chapters 9 and 10), as does the question of whether the species represented here are equally selective in their auditory response to the various maternal calls (see chapter 4).

Since altricial forms have not been studied, it is not known whether audition predominates over vision early in development in these species. Such a study also could significantly augment our knowledge of the sequential development of the sensory systems in birds (Gottlieb 1968b). At present almost all of our knowledge about the prenatal development of the sensory systems comes from the domestic chick embryo, which is a circumstance to be deplored. So far the chick embryo has been the favorite subject for the study of avian behavioral embryology for much the same reasons that the white rat has dominated studies in experimental psychology: convenience, convention, and cost. As Lockard (1968) has shown, many of the various strains of laboratory rats are freaks; we must be alert to the possibility that the domestic chick embryo may also be a freak in certain respects. In any event the extension of avian behavioral embryology to species other than the chick would seem to be desirable, especially from a comparative point of view.

Summary
Species-specific maternal auditory stimulation is more potent (attractive) than species-specific visual stimulation in all

species tested (domestic chicks, domestic ducklings, wild mallard ducklings, and wild wood ducklings). Thus, this generalization holds for wild and domestic forms as well as hole-nesting and ground-nesting species. Since all the forms tested are precocial, it is not yet known whether this conclusion also holds for altricial species.

4

Species-Specific Nature of Auditory Perception: Tests with Single Calls

THE previous experiments demonstrated that maternally naive chicks and ducklings are more attracted to the auditory than to the visual component of a hen of their own species. The next question concerns the selectivity of the birds' response to maternal calls of various species.

There are several evolutionary or ethological hypotheses concerning the specificity of behavior, the most notable of which stems from Lorenz's (1940) observation that the behavior of adult wild birds is in some respects more highly specific than that of domestic ones. According to Lorenz's theory, domestication is associated with a relative loss in species-specific behavior because artificial selection tends to relax or change the breeding and survival patterns which favor the evolution and maintenance of specificity under natural conditions. There can be no question that this assumption is correct; artificial selection *does* change breeding and survival patterns. Whether any losses in the specificity of behavior are a direct consequence of artificial selection is not known, however. In other words, there may be a relative loss in the species-specificity of behavior in adult domestic animals, but not for the reason cited by Lorenz. For example, ontogenetic factors could play a very important role in any loss of behavioral specificity in adult animals, especially when one considers the vast difference in wild and domestic rearing environments. In the context of the present experiments, the artificial vs. natural selection hypothesis would predict that the domestic chicks and ducklings either would not exhibit a selective response to the maternal call of their own species or, if they did, it would be less pronounced than their wild counterparts.

Another hypothesis (Fabricius 1951) would predict that hole-nesting ducklings may be more highly specific in the auditory perception of their own species' maternal call than are ground-nesting ducklings. This prediction rests on the assumption that hole-nesting birds are more dependent upon auditory stimulation from the parent than ground-nesting species because of ecological differences in nesting site (Fabricius 1951, Klopfer 1959). While the previous experiment (chapter 3) did not support this particular assumption, it still could be the case that wood ducklings are more selective than mallard ducklings in their response to maternal calls of various species.

To shed light on the above questions, in the present experiments domestic white rock chicks and peking ducklings, and wild wood ducks and mallards, were exposed to the maternal calls of various species emanating from a non-visible sound source (auditory test). In the first experiment, the birds were exposed to stationary calls (approach-response) and in the second experiment other birds were exposed to moving calls (following-response). Each bird was exposed to only one call, that of its own species or some other species. All the birds were tested between 10 to 40 hours after hatching.

While the choice of the maternal calls to which the birds were exposed was based partly on availability, attention is drawn to the fact that the most ethologically relevant comparisons can be made by comparing the peking and mallard ducklings' response to the mallard and pintail calls (same genus, *Anas*) and the wood ducklings' response to the wood duck and mandarin calls (same genus, *Aix*). The peking duck is a highly domesticated mallard form, so it is particularly pertinent in the present context to compare the peking and mallard ducklings' response to the mallard maternal call.

Results

As shown in tables 6 and 9, the domestic white rock chicks responded only to their own species' maternal call in both the approach and following tests. While the domestic peking ducklings showed a relatively high level of responsiveness (percent responded) to all the maternal calls in the approach test, they showed a significantly higher level of responsiveness to their own species maternal call (mallard) in the following test.

As shown in tables 6 and 9, the wood ducklings showed a similar level of responsiveness to all the maternal calls in the approach test, and a significantly elevated response to their own species maternal call in the following test. The mallards showed a higher level of responsiveness to the mallard, pintail, and chicken calls than to the wood duck and mandarin calls in the approach test. In the following test, in terms of statistical reliability, the mallards failed to show a higher response to their own species' maternal call vs. the pintail, wood duck, and chicken calls, though they did show a significantly higher response to the mallard call than to the mandarin call.

On the question of the effects of domestication, a further relevant comparison can be made between the mallards and pekings since they are wild and domestic counterparts of the same species. In the approach test (table 6), the mallards showed a significantly higher incidence of response to the

TABLE 6

Approach-Response of Domestic Chicks, Peking, Mallard, and Wood Ducklings Exposed to Maternal Calls of Mallard, Pintail, Wood Duck, Mandarin, and Chicken during Four-Minute Approach Test

Species Tested	Mallard	S.D.	Pintail	S.D.	Wood Duck	S.D.	Mandarin	S.D.	Chicken	S.D.
					MATERNAL CALLS					
Chicks	(N = 15)				(N = 15)				(N = 25)	
Percent responded	0		...		0		...		72	
Ave. latency (sec.)	...		...		...		...		98.1	52.3
Ave. duration (sec.)	...		...		...		...		111.0	44.4
Pekings	(N = 25)		(N = 25)		(N = 25)		(N = 25)		(N = 25)	
Percent responded	76		80		60		28		56	
Ave. latency (sec.)	47.4	45.2	100.5	58.1	54.5	52.8	75.4	59.4	73.6	36.2
Ave. duration (sec.)	136.3	65.2	95.7	47.6	106.7	53.5	90.7	65.7	113.2	76.5
Mallards	(N = 21)		(N = 20)		(N = 20)		(N = 20)		(N = 20)	
Percent responded	81		80		40		25		75	
Ave. latency (sec.)	44.9	50.5	53.0	63.6	48.0	73.3	47.6	47.8	55.5	31.3
Ave. duration (sec.)	137.0	65.7	95.4	59.5	59.8	40.6	30.4	27.5	138.9	69.6
Wood ducks	(N = 20)		(N = 22)		(N = 21)		(N = 21)		(N = 20)	
Percent responded	50		45		62		67		60	
Ave. latency (sec.)	47.2	70.1	60.8	59.0	36.6	36.8	28.5	24.5	49.6	39.1
Ave. duration (sec.)	120.8	93.7	35.3	28.3	103.3	70.6	139.5	81.0	76.3	73.7

NOTE: No chicks were tested for their response to the pintail and mandarin calls. See tables 7 and 8 for statistical analysis.

TABLE 7

Statistical Analysis of the Peking Duckling and Mallard Duckling
Approach-Response Data in Table 6

Species	Maternal Calls	p Value (2-tailed)
	Incidence of Response	
Pekings	mallard and wood duck	ns
Pekings	mallard and chicken	ns
Pekings	mallard and mandarin	.004
Pekings	pintail and chicken	ns
Pekings	pintail and wood duck	ns
Pekings	mandarin and pintail	.002
Pekings	wood duck and mandarin	.04
Pekings	mandarin and chicken	.08
Mallards	mallard and wood duck	.01
Mallards	mallard and mandarin	.001
Mallards	pintail and mandarin	.002
Mallards	wood duck and chicken	.06
Mallards	pintail and wood duck	.02
Mallards	mandarin and chicken	.006
Pekings and mallards	wood duck	ns
Pekings and mallards	chicken	ns
	Latency of Response (responders only)	
Pekings	mallard and pintail	<.001
Pekings	mallard and chicken	.01
Pekings	mallard and mandarin	ns
Pekings	wood duck and chicken	.08
Pekings	mandarin and pintail	ns
Pekings	pintail and wood duck	.01
Pekings	wood duck and mandarin	ns
Mallards	wood duck and chicken	.08
Pekings and mallards	wood duck	ns
Pekings and mallards	pintail	.008
Pekings and mallards	chicken	ns
Pekings and mallards	mandarin	ns
	Duration of Response (responders only)	
Pekings	mallard and pintail	.04
Pekings	mallard and mandarin	ns

(Table 7 continued)

Species	Maternal Calls	p Value (2-tailed)
Pekings	mallard and chicken	*ns*
Pekings	mallard and wood duck	*ns*
Pekings	pintail and chicken	*ns*
Pekings	mandarin and chicken	*ns*
Pekings	wood duck and mandarin	*ns*
Mallards	mallard and pintail	.08
Mallards	mallard and wood duck	.006
Mallards	mallard and mandarin	.002
Mallards	pintail and mandarin	.01
Mallards	chicken and wood duck	.006
Mallards	chicken and pintail	.04
Mallards	pintail and wood duck	*ns*
Mallards	wood duck and mandarin	.08
Mallards	mandarin and chicken	.004
Pekings and mallards	wood duck	.04
Pekings and mallards	chicken	*ns*
Pekings and mallards	mandarin	.04

ns = nonsignificant statistical difference (two-tailed $p > .10$).

TABLE 8
Statistical Analysis of the Wood Duckling and Mallard Duckling
Approach-Response Data in Table 6

Species	Maternal Calls	p Value (2-tailed)
	Incidence of Response	
Wood ducks	wood duck and pintail	*ns*
Wood ducks	mandarin and pintail	*ns*
Mallards	mallard and wood duck	.01
Mallards	mallard and mandarin	.001
Mallards	wood duck and chicken	.06
Mallards	mandarin and pintail	.002
Mallards	mandarin and chicken	.006
Mallards	wood duck and pintail	.02
Wood ducks and mallards	mallard	.08
Wood ducks and mallards	wood duck	*ns*
Wood ducks and mallards	mandarin	.01
Wood ducks and mallards	pintail	.04

(Table 8 continued)

Species	Maternal Calls	p Value (2-tailed)
	Latency of Response (responders only)	
Wood ducks	wood duck and pintail	*ns*
Wood ducks	mallard and mandarin	*ns*
Wood ducks	mandarin and pintail	*ns*
Wood ducks	mandarin and chicken	*ns*
Mallards	pintail and wood duck	.06
Mallards	wood duck and chicken	.08
Mallards ·	mandarin and chicken	*ns*
Wood ducks and mallards	mandarin	*ns*
	Duration of Response (responders only)	
Wood ducks	wood duck and pintail	.006
Wood ducks	wood duck and mandarin	*ns*
Wood ducks	wood duck and chicken	*ns*
Wood ducks	mandarin and pintail	.004
Wood ducks	mallard and chicken	*ns*
Wood ducks	mandarin and chicken	.06
Wood ducks	mallard and pintail	.04
Wood ducks	pintail and chicken	*ns*
Mallards	mallard and pintail	.08
Mallards	mallard and wood duck	.006
Mallards	mallard and mandarin	.002
Mallards	pintail and mandarin	.01
Mallards	pintail and wood duck	*ns*
Mallards	wood duck and chicken	.006
Mallards	mandarin and chicken	.004
Mallards	wood duck and mandarin	.08
Mallards	pintail and chicken	.04
Wood ducks and mallards	wood duck	*ns*
Wood ducks and mallards	mandarin	.02
Wood ducks and mallards	mallard	*ns*
Wood ducks and mallards	pintail	.004
Wood ducks and mallards	chicken	.04

ns = nonsignificant statistical difference (two-tailed *p* > .10).

59

TABLE 9

Following-Response of Domestic Chicks, Peking, Mallard, and Wood Ducklings Exposed to Maternal Calls of Mallard, Pintail, Wood Duck, Mandarin, and Chicken during Twenty-Minute Following Test

SPECIES TESTED	MATERNAL CALLS									
	Mallard	S.D.	Pintail	S.D.	Wood Duck	S.D.	Mandarin	S.D.	Chicken	S.D.
Chicks	(N = 15)				(N = 15)				(N = 25)	
Percent responded	0		…		0				92	
Ave. latency (sec.)	…		…		…				300.4	228.8
Ave. duration (sec.)	…		…		…				173.5	108.9
Pekings	(N = 25)		(N = 20)		(N = 20)		(N = 25)		(N = 20)	
Percent responded	52		10		10		0		15	
Ave. latency (sec.)	331.9	297.1	84.5	68.6	218.5	194.5	…		651.0	435.7
Ave. duration (sec.)	121.9	165.1	244.0	147.1	385.0	516.2	…		99.0	88.5
Mallards	(N = 20)		(N = 20)		(N = 20)		(N = 22)		(N = 20)	
Percent responded	50		55		25		9		25	
Ave. latency (sec.)	193.5	270.6	227.3	152.7	306.2	259.2	704.0	374.8	110.2	45.0
Ave. duration (sec.)	98.5	94.7	53.3	33.5	29.8	37.0	33.0	28.3	98.4	100.0
Wood ducks	(N = 20)				(N = 33)				(N = 20)	
Percent responded	25		…		61				20	
Ave. latency (sec.)	271.8	233.3	…		78.7	84.5	…		105.8	34.0
Ave. duration (sec.)	20.4	7.2	…		79.4	76.0	…		58.8	25.6

NOTE: No chicks or wood ducks were tested for their response to the pintail and mandarin calls. See tables 10 and 11 for statistical analysis of following-response data.

mallard call than to the wood duck and mandarin calls, and no difference in the incidence of their response to the mallard and pintail or chicken calls. In the approach test, more of the pekings responded to the mallard call than to the mandarin call; otherwise the incidence of their response to the mallard and the other calls was not different. The mallards approached all of the calls equally fast (latency), while the pekings responded more slowly to the pintail and chicken calls than to the mallard call. The mallards showed a greater duration of approach to the mallard call than to the pintail, wood duck, and mandarin calls, while the pekings showed a longer duration of approach only to the mallard vs. pintail calls.

In the following test (table 9), more of the mallards followed the mallard call than the mandarin call; otherwise the mallards were equally responsive to all the calls relative to the mallard call. More of the pekings responded to the mallard call than to any of the other calls. The pekings and mallards followed the mallard call with equal strength (incidence, latency, and duration of response). So few pekings followed the other calls, it is inadvisable to make comparisons between the Pekings and mallards on latency and duration of response to calls other than the mallard.

The statistical analysis of the data in table 6 (approach-response) is shown in tables 7 and 8, while the statistical analysis of the data in table 9 (following-response) is shown in tables 10 and 11.

Discussion

On the question of the effects of domestication on species-specific behavior, the results suggest that, if anything, there has been an increase in specificity as a consequence of domestication, at least with respect to the auditory perception of species. The most highly domesticated form in the current experiments, the domestic white rock chick, showed absolute specificity of its response to the maternal call of its

TABLE 10

Statistical Analysis of the Peking and Mallard Following-Response Data in Table 9

Species	Maternal Calls	p value (2-tailed)
Incidence of Response		
Pekings	mallard and wood duck	.01
Pekings	mallard and mandarin	$<$.01
Pekings	mallard and chicken	.02
Pekings	mallard and pintail	.01
Mallards	mallard and pintail	ns
Mallards	mallard and wood duck	ns
Mallards	mallard and mandarin	.01
Mallards	mallard and chicken	ns
Mallards	pintail and mandarin	.006
Mallards	pintail and chicken	.10
Mallards	pintail and wood duck	ns
Pekings and mallards	mallard	ns
Pekings and mallards	pintail	.008
Pekings and mallards	wood duck	ns
Latency of Response (responders only)		
Pekings	mallard and pintail	ns
Pekings	mallard and wood duck	ns
Pekings	mallard and chicken	ns
Pekings	pintail and wood duck	ns
Pekings	pintail and chicken	ns
Pekings	wood duck and chicken	ns
Mallards	mallard and pintail	ns
Mallards	mallard and wood duck	ns
Mallards	mallard and mandarin	.06
Mallards	mallard and chicken	ns
Mallards	pintail and mandarin	.02
Mallards	pintail and chicken	ns
Mallards	wood duck and chicken	ns
Mallards	pintail and wood duck	ns
Mallards	wood duck and mandarin	.06
Mallards	mandarin and chicken	.03
Pekings and mallards	mallard	ns
Pekings and mallards	pintail	ns
Pekings and mallards	wood duck	ns
Pekings and mallards	chicken	.02

(Table 10 continued)

Species	Maternal Calls	p value (2-tailed)
	Duration of Response (responders only)	
Pekings	mallard and wood duck	ns
Pekings	mallard and chicken	ns
Pekings	pintail and wood duck	ns
Pekings	pintail and chicken	ns
Pekings	wood duck and chicken	ns
Pekings	mallard and pintail	ns
Mallards	mallard and pintail	ns
Mallards	mallard and wood duck	.01
Mallards	mallard and mandarin	ns
Mallards	mallard and chicken	ns
Mallards	wood duck and chicken	ns
Mallards	pintail and chicken	ns
Mallards	pintail and mandarin	ns
Mallards	pintail and wood duck	.08
Mallards	mandarin and chicken	ns
Pekings and mallards	mallard	ns
Pekings and mallards	pintail	.04
Pekings and mallards	wood duck	ns

ns — statistically unreliable (two-tailed p>.10).

own species; this absolute specificity was not present in the domestic or wild ducklings, nor in the hole-nesting ducklings. In contrasting the behavior of the wild mallards and domestic mallards (pekings), both showed a relative specificity for the mallard call, with the mallards being somewhat more specific in their approach-response and the pekings being more specific in their following-response. When the pekings and mallards are compared in their response to the pintail call, the difference is exactly opposite to that which would be predicted from the domestication hypothesis. Namely, the pekings showed more evidence of specificity than did the mallards. Though there was no difference in the proportion of pekings and mallards which approached the mallard and pintail calls, the pekings showed a longer latency and a shorter duration of approach to the pintail vs. the mallard calls, while the mallards showed only a shorter duration of approach to the pintail call. In the following test, the mallards were equally responsive to the mallard and pintail calls, while the pekings were significantly less responsive to the pintail call than they were to the mallard call. Thus, in what was perhaps the most crucial test between the domestic and wild mallards, domestication (artificial selection) has

TABLE 11
Statistical Analysis of the Wood Duck and Mallard Following-Response Data in Table 9

Species	Maternal Calls	p Value (2-tailed)
Incidence of Response		
Wood ducks	wood duck and mallard	.02
Wood ducks	wood duck and chicken	.01
Mallards	mallard and chicken	ns
Mallards	mallard and wood duck	ns
Wood ducks and mallards	mallard	ns
Wood ducks and mallards	wood duck	.02
Wood ducks and mallards	chicken	ns
Latency of Response (responders only)		
Wood ducks	mallard and wood duck	.01
Wood ducks	mallard and chicken	.08
Wood ducks	wood duck and chicken	ns
Mallards	mallard and chicken	ns
Mallards	mallard and wood duck	ns
Wood ducks and mallards	mallard	ns
Wood ducks and mallards	wood duck	.08
Wood ducks and mallards	chicken	ns
Duration of Response (responders only)		
Wood ducks	mallard and chicken	.02
Wood ducks	mallard and wood duck	.08
Wood ducks	wood duck and chicken	ns
Wood ducks and mallards	mallard	.01
Wood ducks and mallards	wood duck	.06
Wood ducks and mallards	chicken	ns

ns = statistically unreliable (two-tailed $p > .10$).

served to sharpen the species-specificity of auditory perception. Since mallard ducklings evince more fearful behavior than peking ducklings under the same test conditions (Gottlieb 1961), it is possible that the reduced specificity of the mallards is a consequence of their heightened fear level (i.e., the pekings outperform the mallards because they are less fearful in this situation). If this is the case, artificial selection, by reducing the level of fear in peking ducklings relative to mallards, has indirectly served to sharpen the specificity of their performance under the present conditions. The present suggestion, however, allows no inferences about the role that artificial selection may have played in differences observed in the adult behavior of wild and domestic forms. When differences in the species-specificity of behavior are observed in wild and domestic forms, especially in adult courting and mating behavior (Lorenz 1940), the possibility that such differences are partially attributable to ontogenetic and intercurrent environmental differences between the two forms must also be considered.

Regarding the relationship of hole-nesting or ground-nesting to specificity of response to the various maternal calls, the mallards showed greater specificity than the wood ducklings in the approach test, and the wood ducklings showed greater specificity than the mallards in the following test. (In the following test, they could be compared only on the three calls to which the wood ducklings were exposed.) Thus, the present evidence does not support the notion of greater species-specificity of auditory perception in hole-nesting species: the approach-response shows that the ground-nesting mallards are more specific than the hole-nesting wood ducklings and, the following-response, that the wood ducklings are more specific than the mallards. If one considers the following-response to be a more critical measure than the approach-response, then it should be noted that the wood ducklings followed the mallard and chicken calls no less strongly (incidence, latency, duration) than the mallards followed the wood duck and chicken calls. The difference that exists is between the wood ducklings' response to the wood duck call relative to the other two calls and the mallards' response to the mallard call relative to the other two calls. If the number of mallards ($N = 20$) exposed to the mallard call had been as large as the number of wood ducklings exposed to the wood duck call ($N = 33$), it is probable that the differences between the mallards' response to the mallard call vs. the other two calls would have been statistically reliable.

Generally speaking, the approach test was not as revealing as the following test with respect to the selective nature of the birds' response to the various calls. That is, with the exception of the mallards, all the species showed their strongest response to their own maternal call in the following test, whether or not they did so in the approach test. From the perceptual standpoint, it is very interesting to note that the pekings, mallards, and wood ducklings showed as high a level of approach responsiveness to the chicken maternal call as they did to their own species maternal call, whereas the chicks were totally unresponsive to the mallard and wood duck maternal calls.

Summary

When the birds are presented with a single call (rather than two calls simultaneously), the domestic chicks show the highest degree of species-specificity both in the approach- and following-response. The ducklings approach a wider variety of calls than they will follow, and the following-response generally brings out the species-specificity of the birds' response.

Based on the present test conditions, domestication has not weakened the species-specificity of auditory perception. Also, the preference for hole-nesting is not associated with a higher degree of species-specific auditory perception than is ground-nesting.

5

Species-Specific Nature
of Auditory Perception
in Simultaneous Choice Tests

FROM the results of the last experiments one can conclude
that the ducklings will more readily approach a greater number of calls than they will follow and that the following-
response is perhaps a better measure of the potency or
attractiveness of an auditory stimulus than is the approach-
response. As the present experiments will show, however,
the approach-response can be a highly discriminative
measure when it is employed in a simultaneous choice situation. It is only in the case of tests utilizing a single call
(rather than two calls simultaneously) that the approach-
response is a poor measure of perceptual preference. At the
methodological level, use of the single-call method or the
simultaneous choice procedure depends upon whether one
wishes to determine the range of stimuli which will be
approached (single-call method) or whether one wants to
get a satisfactory measure of preference or discriminative
ability (simultaneous choice procedure). The present experiments also demonstrate the importance of immediate field
or contextual factors in the study of behavior (Kuo 1967).

FIVE

As will be seen, both the level and direction of responsiveness of the birds is influenced by the particular calls which are present in the simultaneous-choice tests.

In addition to clarifying the methodological problems associated with different testing conditions, the present chapter also sheds more definitive light on the question of domestication, as well as the relationship of hole-nesting and ground-nesting to specificity of auditory perception. For example, while the pekings and mallards are more or less equally responsive to the mallard and pintail maternal calls in the single-call approach test, the more crucial question concerns their preference when presented with both calls simultaneously. The same question holds true for the wood ducklings' response in a simultaneous choice between the wood duck and mandarin maternal calls. To examine these questions in greater detail, peking and mallard ducklings were tested with the mallard vs. pintail and mallard vs. wood duck maternal calls, and the wood ducklings were tested with the wood duck vs. mandarin, wood duck vs. mallard, and wood duck vs. chicken maternal calls.

Since the domestic white rock chicks showed absolute specificity in their approach-response to the various maternal calls in the single-call method (previous chapter), to add substance to the methodological issues raised in the first paragraph above, domestic white rock chicks were tested with the chicken vs. mallard and chicken vs. wood duck maternal calls. From the chicks' performance in the single-call approach test, one might predict that in the simultaneous choice tests the chicks' responsiveness would be relatively high, and that it would be restricted solely to the chicken maternal call. If these predictions are not correct, then the influence of the contextual element in the simultaneous choice tests would be underscored as an important methodological item. As a precursor to later experiments, in the present one the chicks were also exposed to a simultaneous choice test between the chicken maternal call and the chick brooding-like call. The latter call is one which the chicks have heard prior to testing, both through self-emission and through the vocalizations of other chicks. If it is simply a matter of approaching the familiar call in these tests, the chicks should choose the chick call. As shown in the audio-spectrographic analyses of the calls (chapter 2), the fundamental frequencies of the chicken maternal call (775 Hz) and the chick brooding-like call (3,600 Hz) are quite dissimilar.

Results

For the reader's convenience a summary of the birds' performance in the simultaneous auditory choice tests is presented in table 12 (chicks) and table 14 (ducklings). For those interested in the details (actual latency and duration of response to each call in all the tests), this information is shown in table 13 for the chicks and table 15 for the ducklings.

As indicated in tables 12 and 13, the chicks showed a strong preference for the chicken maternal call in all the simultaneous choice tests. The level of responsiveness varied somewhat between the tests (though this was statistically unreliable in all cases), and it was considerably lower than

---

TABLE 12
Auditory Preferences of Chicks in Simultaneous Choice Tests between Chicken Maternal Call, Maternal Calls of Other Species, and Chick Brooding-Like Call during Four-Minute Approach Test

Test Calls	N	Responded no.	%	Preference no.	%
Chicken vs. chick	25	13/25 =	52	12/13 =	92 chicken
				1/13 =	8 chick
Chicken vs. mallard	25	7/25 =	28	7/7 =	100 chicken
Chicken vs. wood duck	25	11/25 =	44	9/11 =	82 chicken
				2/11 =	18 wood duck

NOTE: See table 13 for latency and duration of response to each of the calls.

TABLE 13

Latency and Duration of Response of Chicks in Simultaneous Choice Tests between Chicken Maternal Call, Maternal Calls of Other Species, and Chick Brooding-like Call during Four-Minute Approach Test

Test Calls	N	Latency (sec.)				Duration (sec.)			
		Chicken		Other		Chicken		Other	
		M	S.D.	M	S.D.	M	S.D.	M	S.D.
Chicken vs. chick	25	120.4	79.4	228.6	41.0	80.9	58.2	2.1	7.5
Chicken vs. mallard	25	83.9	69.2	219.0	55.6	76.1	29.9	4.1	10.9
Chicken vs. wood duck	25	129.9	76.9	206.8	73.8	68.0	53.8	19.4	47.7

NOTE: See table 12.

the chicks' responsiveness to the chicken maternal call in the single-call approach test (previous chapter). Also, some of the chicks responded to the wood duck maternal call in the simultaneous choice test whereas none responded to the wood duck maternal call in the single-call tests in the previous experiment. In the chicken vs. chick call test, the chicks strongly preferred the maternal call.

As can be seen in table 14, the pekings and mallards both showed a very high level of discrimination of the mallard maternal call in the various simultaneous choice tests. The wood ducklings, on the other hand, showed little or no evidence of discrimination in the tests involving the wood duck vs. mallard or wood duck vs. chicken maternal calls. In the wood duck vs. mandarin test, however, the wood ducklings showed a preference for the wood duck maternal call.

The details (incidence, latency, and duration of response) of the ducklings' performance in the various choice tests is shown in table 15. It is of interest that more of the pekings responded ($p = .02$) in the mallard vs. pintail test than in the mallard vs. wood duck test, and the pekings' response to the mallard was prompter ($p < .02$) in the former test as compared to the latter one. However, there was no difference in the duration of the pekings' response in the mallard vs. wood duck and mallard vs. pintail tests. Also, more of the mallards than pekings responded ($p = .08$) in the mallard vs. wood duck test, and the mallards' response to the mallard call was swifter ($p = .02$) than the pekings' response to the mallard call in that test. In the 4-minute mallard vs. wood duck test in which the wood ducklings showed some evidence of a preference for the wood duck call, their response to the wood duck call was faster ($p = .002$) and of longer duration ($p = .004$) than to the mallard call, thereby supporting the impression of a preference in that particular test. Why the wood ducklings should have failed to demonstrate a preference for the wood duck call in the 5-minute

TABLE 14
Auditory Preferences of Ducklings in Simultaneous Choice Tests

Species	Maternal Calls	N	Responded no. %	Preference no. %
Peking	mallard vs. wood duck[b]	44	27/44 = 61	24/27 = 89 mallard 3/27 = 11 wood duck
Peking	mallard vs. pintail[b]	21	19/21 = 90	19/19 = 100 mallard
Mallard	mallard vs. wood duck[b]	22	19/22 = 86	18/19 = 95 mallard 1/19 = 5 wood duck
Mallard	mallard vs. pintail[a]	20	19/20 = 95	18/19 = 95 mallard 1/19 = 5 pintail
Wood duck	wood duck vs. mallard[a]	15	12/15 = 80	7/12 = 58 wood duck 3/12 = 25 mallard
Wood duck	wood duck vs. mallard[b]	20	16/20 = 80	6/16 = 37 wood duck 7/16 = 44 mallard
Wood duck	wood duck vs. mandarin[b]	20	16/20 = 80	12/16 = 75 wood duck 1/16 = 6 mandarin
Wood duck	wood duck vs. chicken[a]	15	11/15 = 73	5/11 = 45 wood duck 5/11 = 45 chicken

NOTE: In certain instances the preference percentages total less than 100 because all responding animals did not show a preference between the two calls as defined in chapter 2. See table 15 for latency and duration of response to each of the calls. [a] 4-minute approach test. [b] 5-minute approach test.

TABLE 15

Latency and Duration of Responses of Ducklings in Simultaneous Choice Tests

Species	Maternal Calls	N	Latency (sec.)				Duration (sec.)			
			M	S.D.	M	S.D.	M	S.D.	M	S.D.
			Mallard		**Other**		**Mallard**		**Other**	
Peking	mallard vs. wood duck[t]	44	108.0	89.3	276.0	72.4	144.6	87.2	22.7	68.0
Peking	mallard vs. pintail[b]	21	68.2	55.7	300.0	0.0	177.8	79.2	0.0	0.0
Mallard	mallard vs. wood duck[a]	22	62.2	72.7	295.5	19.5	140.8	87.4	4.5	19.5
Mallard	mallard vs. pintail[a]	20	50.4	59.9	217.5	58.7	130.7	67.1	2.7	6.8
Wood duck	mallard vs. wood duck[a]	15	170.2	88.9	56.8	87.5	11.6	15.2	77.4	76.0
Wood duck	mallard vs. wood duck[a]	20	135.4	114.5	155.9	120.9	60.0	71.3	45.6	59.2
			Mandarin		**Wood Duck**		**Mandarin**		**Wood Duck**	
Wood duck	mandarin vs. wood duck[b]	20	251.0	100.1	77.6	87.7	6.9	12.7	74.9	74.3
			Chicken		**Wood Duck**		**Chicken**		**Wood Duck**	
Wood duck	chicken vs. wood duck[a]	15	126.7	99.1	97.6	113.3	59.5	67.9	70.6	81.8

NOTE: See table 14.

In those cases where a bird's response was restricted solely to one of the calls, a latency of 240 sec. (4-min. test) or 300 sec. (5-min. test) was assigned to the other call. In such cases, a 0.0-sec. duration score was also assigned to the other call. In those cases where a bird did not respond to either call, the bird was omitted from the tabulation of latency and duration of response. These methods of tabulating latency and duration of response hold for all simultaneous choice tests reported in this monograph. In single choice tests, the latency and duration data include only those birds which responded. [a] 4-minute approach test. [b] 5-minute approach test.

wood duck vs. mallard test is not at all clear, but these results do suggest that caution must be exercised in interpret-
ing the wood ducklings' behavior in the mallard vs. wood
duck test. Our impression of the wood ducklings over the
years has been that their behavior is generally more variable
than the mallards' or pekings' in a laboratory situation.

Discussion

The discriminative value of using the approach-response
in the simultaneous choice procedure is evident when one
compares the approach-response of the pekings and mallards
to the pintail maternal call presented by itself (previous
chapter) and in simultaneous opposition to the mallard
maternal call (this chapter). In the former case the birds
showed a strong approach-response to both calls, but when
the calls are placed in simultaneous opposition there is clear
evidence of the birds' preference for the mallard call. In
addition to indicating the birds' preference for the mallard
call, this finding also indicates their ability to discriminate
the mallard call in the presence of another call to which they
are strongly attracted under other circumstances. Therefore,
the approach-response can be used as a discriminative
measure of the birds' behavior under simultaneous choice
conditions, whereas the single-call method taps the range
of stimuli which the bird will approach. As shown in the
previous experiment, the following-response usually provides
a better preference index than the approach-response when
the single-call method is used. However, according to the
present results, the approach-response in the simultaneous
choice procedure is an even better measure of discrimination
or preference than the following-response to a single call.
For example, the mallards followed the pintail call as
strongly as they followed the mallard call in the single-call
test (table 9, chapter 4), but in the simultaneous approach
test the mallards showed a very strong preference for the
mallard call over the pintail call (tables 14 and 15). Because

of these considerations, the 4- or 5-minute simultaneous approach test would seem to be the best and the stiffest single procedure for determining the birds' auditory preferences and/or discriminative abilities. Under these conditions it is obvious that if a bird exhibits a clear preference for one of the calls, it must be able to discriminate it from the other call. The absence of a clear preference in the simultaneous choice test means that the birds (as a group) may not have a preference between the calls or that they do have a preference but are unable to manifest it because of an inability to discriminate between the calls. (Whether *any* preferences exist can be determined by the single-call procedure.) Thus, the *operational* specificity of the birds' auditory perception is very high when they can discriminate their own species' maternal call in a simultaneous choice situation, and the operational specificity of the birds' auditory perception of their species' maternal call is low when they cannot discriminate it under simultaneous choice conditions.

The discussion above was a necessary prelude to reaching a conclusion about the performance of the ducklings and chicks in the present experiment. Since all of the duck species tested do have a preference for the maternal call of their own species as indicated by their approach- and/or following-response in the single-call test, we can conclude from the present results that the wood ducklings have a generally lower operational specificity than the mallards (or the pekings) in the auditory perception of their own maternal call. Thus, the hole-nesting propensity of wood ducks is not associated with a greater operational specificity of auditory perception of species than in ground-nesting species. Further, there are no differences in operational specificity between the pekings and mallards — both are highly selective in their response to the mallard maternal call under similar conditions. It is of some interest that more of the mallards responded in the mallard vs. wood duck test, and those which responded did so faster than the pekings. However, there was no difference between the mallards and pekings in the duration of approach to the mallard call in the mallard vs. wood duck test. Both groups were highly specific and responded equally well to the mallard call in the mallard vs. pintail test, which is very significant considering the birds' attraction to the pintail call in the single-call test. Thus, we see no breakdown in the species-specific nature of auditory perception in these young birds as a consequence of domestication. Although Lorenz's (1940) domestication hypothesis may be true for other aspects of duck behavior, especially adult behavior, it still remains to be demonstrated that domestic and wild birds of the same species, *reared under the same conditions,* would in fact show significant differences in species-specific behavior. At the present time it seems equally tenable to suppose that the social behavior of domestic birds is partially a consequence of the crowded conditions of the barnyard and/or human contact, and that the social behavior of wild ducks is in some way attributable to the relatively more isolated cohabitation with wild members of their own and other species. When one considers the great difference in external morphology between wild and domestic ducks, there can be no question that artificial and natural selection have caused a tremendous external morphological divergence in such groups. Whether species-specific behavioral differences mediated by the brain and nervous system have also occurred as a consequence of artificial selection remains to be demonstrated. The only behavioral differences which have been demonstrated experimentally in wild and domestic ducks is a higher level and earlier onset of fear in young mallards in comparison with pekings of the same age (Gottlieb 1961), and the prompter response of mallards to their maternal call under certain test conditions. One does not doubt the possibility that differences in artificial and natural selection can cause a number of significant behavioral differences in ducks — the question is whether the behavioral differences observed by Lorenz (1940) in adult ducks were actually or solely a consequence of artificial selection.

Summary

The simultaneous auditory approach test (i.e., simultaneous presentation of two different maternal calls) is a powerful method for determining the chicks' and ducklings' ability to select the proper call. The chicks, pekings, and mallards showed a very high ability to discriminate their maternal call under all conditions. Under these circumstances, the wood ducklings are less able than the ground-nesting species to discriminate the maternal call of their own species.

6

Species-Specific Nature of Visual Perception in Peking and Mallard Ducklings

IN the previous chapters it has been demonstrated that white rock chicks, peking ducklings, mallard ducklings, and wood ducklings are more responsive to the auditory component of their maternal parent than to the visual component, and that these species are generally able to distinguish the maternal call of their own species from that of certain other species.

The next question to be examined concerns the ability of peking and mallard ducklings to distinguish the visual attributes of their maternal parent from the visual attributes of parents of other species. As was shown in chapter 3, under the present conditions, the ducklings are much less responsive to the sheerly visual component than they are to the auditory component of their maternal parent. This low level of response has been a serious obstacle in our attempt to evaluate the species-specific visual discrimination abilities of the species represented in the present work. In previous experiments (Gottlieb 1961), conducted under different conditions, a larger proportion of pekings and mallards followed a sheerly visual object (male mallard decoy) than do so under the present conditions. The previous apparatus, although it was a circular open field like the present one, was somewhat smaller in circumference and it had a much lighter and more heterogeneous background (Gottlieb 1961, fig. 1) than the present totally black apparatus (fig. 2 in chapter 2). Although one can not be certain that the black background is the feature which is responsible for the relatively lower level of response to visual objects in the present apparatus, it is the most conspicuous difference between the present apparatus and the one used previously. (It is also of interest that, when one surveys the visual imprinting literature, most workers have used an apparatus which has a relatively light background. It is not possible to say whether this has occurred through design or chance, since there have been no published reports of the influence of background on the approach- or following-response to visual stimuli.)

In any event our attempt to examine the species-specificity of visual perception has been handicapped by the low level of responsiveness to purely visual stimulus objects under the present conditions. In the succeeding chapter it will be seen that auditory stimulation of almost any kind significantly raises the level of response to moving visual objects, and that there are audiovisual interactions which cannot be predicted from a knowledge of the birds' response to the auditory and visual components by themselves.

In the present experiment, 14 to 31 hours after hatching, 122 peking and 84 mallard ducklings were exposed to one of four visual replicas during a 20-minute following test: stuffed peking hen, stuffed mallard hen, male mallard papiermâché decoy, or a stuffed wood duck hen. These stimulus objects differed primarily in color and size (fig. 3 in chapter 2). If the visual attributes of the hen contribute to species-specific perception, both the pekings and mallards should show a significantly lower response to the wood duck hen, and the mallards should be less responsive to the peking hen than to the mallard hen. Since the mallard hen represents the ancestral species from which the domestic peking was derived, peking ducklings were exposed to both the peking and mallard hens. The male mallard is the most brilliantly colored of all the replicas, so it was a matter of interest to determine its attractiveness to the domestic and wild birds. (In nature the male is sometimes present during the nest-departure, but not always.)

Because of the low level of response in visual choice tests under the current conditions, the following-response to the individual objects was used as a measure of preference rather than the approach- or following-response in a simultaneous choice test.

Results

In terms of the proportion of birds which followed in each of the conditions, there was a tendency ($p = .08$) for more of the pekings to follow the mallard hen and the mallard drake than the peking hen (tables 16 and 17) — that is, the pekings tended to be least responsive to the peking hen. The pekings were as responsive to the wood duck hen as they were to the other replicas.

The mallards showed no difference in the proportion which responded to each of the hens (peking, mallard, wood duck). None of the mallards followed the male mallard decoy.

In comparing the performance of the pekings and the mallards under the present conditions, while none of the mallards responded to the male mallard (drake) decoy, 25% of the pekings did respond to it ($p = .06$). The pekings tended ($p = .10$) to follow the mallard hen and the wood duck hen more persistently than the mallards.

Discussion

The present experiment indicated no evidence of species-specificity in the following-response of either the pekings or

TABLE 16

Following-Response of Peking Ducklings and Mallard Ducklings Exposed to Stuffed Peking Hen, Stuffed Mallard Hen, Male Mallard Decoy, and Stuffed Wood Duck Hen during Twenty-Minute Following Test

	VISUAL REPLICAS							
	Stuffed ♀ Peking		Stuffed ♀ Mallard		♂ Mallard Decoy		Stuffed ♀ Wood Duck	
SPECIES TESTED	M	S.D.	M	S.D.	M	S.D.	M	S.D.
Pekings	(N = 30)		(N = 20)		(N = 52)		(N = 20)	
Percent followed	7		30		25		25	
Ave. latency	607.0	151.3	637.3	345.2	680.0	276.9	505.2	306.5
Ave. duration	300.5	181.7	235.7	152.1	264.3	263.1	196.4	127.6
Mallards	(N = 23)		(N = 20)		(N = 20)		(N = 21)	
Percent followed	22		30		0		38	
Ave. latency	581.6	363.7	561.8	211.8	…	…	421.5	188.3
Ave. duration	124.2	128.7	127.8	160.7	…	…	142.6	235.9

NOTE: Latency and duration of following are reported in secs.

TABLE 17
Statistical Analysis of Pekings' and Mallards' Following-Response to Various Visual Replicas

Species	Visual Replicas	p Value (2-tailed)
	Incidence of Response (proportion responded)	
Pekings	stuffed ♀ peking and stuffed ♀ mallard	.08
Pekings	stuffed ♀ peking and stuffed ♀ wood duck	ns
Pekings	stuffed ♀ peking and ♂ mallard decoy	.08
Mallards	stuffed ♀ peking and stuffed ♀ wood duck	ns
Pekings and mallards	stuffed ♀ peking	ns
Pekings and mallards	♂ mallard decoy	.06
Pekings and mallards	stuffed ♀ wood duck	ns
	Latency of Response (responders only)	
Pekings	stuffed ♀ mallard and stuffed ♀ peking	ns
Pekings	stuffed ♀ peking and ♂ mallard decoy	ns
Pekings	stuffed ♀ mallard and stuffed ♀ wood duck	ns
Pekings	stuffed ♀ wood duck and ♂ mallard decoy	ns
Mallards	stuffed ♀ peking and stuffed ♀ wood duck	ns
Mallards	stuffed ♀ mallard and stuffed ♀ wood duck	ns
Pekings and mallards	stuffed ♀ peking	ns
Pekings and mallards	stuffed ♀ mallard	ns
Pekings and mallards	stuffed ♀ wood duck	ns

(Table 17 continued)

	Duration of Response (responders only)	
Pekings	stuffed ♀ mallard and stuffed ♀ wood duck	*ns*
Pekings	stuffed ♀ wood duck and ♂ mallard decoy	*ns*
Pekings	stuffed ♀ mallard and stuffed ♀ peking	*ns*
Pekings	stuffed ♀ peking and ♂ mallard decoy	*ns*
Mallards	stuffed ♀ peking and stuffed ♀ wood duck	*ns*
Mallards	stuffed ♀ mallard and stuffed ♀ wood duck	*ns*
Pekings and mallards	stuffed ♀ peking	*ns*
Pekings and mallards	stuffed ♀ mallard	.10
Pekings and mallards	stuffed ♀ wood duck	.10

NOTE: See table 16. *ns* = two-tailed $p > .10$.

83

mallards with respect to the various visual replicas. It is of interest that the pekings were least responsive to the peking hen, which perhaps indicates the importance of color as an attractant for them (with the exception of its bill, the female peking replica was entirely white; all the replicas were without legs). The main difference between the pekings and mallards was in their response to the male mallard decoy — the pekings were more responsive to it than the mallards. Adult male and female pekings are virtually indistinguishable on visual grounds: the male has a curl in his tail feathers. Adult male and female pekings, like other waterfowl, do have different vocal repertoires, so they can be easily distinguished by auditory cues.

In the absence of specificity in the mallards' and pekings' response to the various nonvocal, visual replicas, it is well to recall that in the wild the auditory component is a normal part of the maternal stimulus configuration during the early stages of development of the maternal–neonate bond. Thus, in the light of the previous experimental results, it can be concluded that the maternal call plays an important energizing and directive role in promoting the following-response to the appropriate object under the usual conditions of stimulation. As shown in chapter 3, the addition of the call to the visual attributes of the hen significantly elevates the proportion of birds which follow the visual replica (energizing effect). The results of the simultaneous auditory choice tests in chapter 4 indicate that the species' maternal call exerts a directive influence on the birds' approach behavior. In the next chapter, we shall take up the question of the effect of various natural and nonnatural audiovisual combinations on the following-response of peking and mallard ducklings.

Summary

No evidence of species-specificity of the following-response was found when the ducklings were presented with the sheerly visual attributes of the various replicas.

7

Species-Specific Nature of Audiovisual Perception in Peking and Mallard Ducklings

IN this chapter we shall examine the question of whether the appropriate maternal call emanating from the appropriate visual replica represents the most effective configuration for elicitation of the following-response. This configuration can be considered the "natural" audiovisual combination insofar as it is the one encountered by the ducklings in nature. To gain some idea of the relative potency of the natural maternal configuration, in the present experiment peking and mallard ducklings were also exposed 10 to 31 hours after hatching to odd or nonnatural audiovisual combinations. In the main experiment there was a total of 8 conditions involving 2 maternal calls and 4 visual replicas. Specifically, either the mallard or the wood duck maternal call emanated from four visual replicas: stuffed mallard hen, stuffed peking hen, stuffed wood duck hen, and a mallard drake decoy. Each of the objects was presented singly during a 20-minute following test, and each duckling was exposed to only 1 of the 8 conditions (as is the case throughout the book).

Results

As can be seen in tables 18 and 19, as far as the pekings are concerned the mallard maternal call instigated a higher proportion of following than the wood duck maternal call regardless of the visual replica with which it was combined. Also, there were no differences between the visual replicas in instigating following (percent followed) when they were combined with the mallard call. In terms of latency of the pekings' following-response, the mallard maternal call emanating from the male mallard decoy was as effective as the mallard call/peking hen combination, and more effective than the mallard call/mallard hen combination. In terms of duration of the pekings' response, a number of different audiovisual combinations were equally effective (mallard call/peking hen, mallard call/male mallard decoy, wood duck call/male mallard decoy, and wood duck call/wood duck hen).

More of the mallard ducklings followed the mallard hen and the wood duck hen when these were combined with the mallard maternal call in contrast to the wood duck maternal call. The mallard call/mallard hen and mallard call/ wood duck hen were equally effective combinations for instigating following and latency of following, while the latter combination promoted a longer duration of following in the mallard ducklings. There were no reliable differences between the peking hen or the male mallard decoy in evoking the mallards' following-response when the mallard call or the wood duck call emanated from these visual replicas. In terms of latency and duration of response, however, the *wood duck* maternal call emanating from the male mallard decoy tended to be the most effective audiovisual combination for the mallards' following-response.

(In describing the results, I have stressed the highlights rather than dwelling on all the possible comparisons which could be made. If the reader has some special question about the results in table 18, he can refer to table 19 to deter-

TABLE 18

Following-Response of Peking and Mallard Ducklings Exposed to Mallard Maternal Call and Wood Duck Maternal Call Emanating from Stuffed Mallard Hen, Stuffed Peking Hen, Male Mallard Decoy, and Stuffed Wood Duck Hen during Twenty-Minute Following Test

	VISUAL REPLICAS															
	Stuffed ♀ Mallard				Stuffed ♀ Peking				♂ Mallard Decoy				Stuffed ♀ Wood Duck			
	Mallard		Wood Duck		Mallard		Wood Duck		Mallard		Wood Duck		Mallard		Wood Duck	
MATERNAL CALLS	M	S.D.	M	S.D.	M	S.D.	M	S.D.	M	S.D.	M	S.D.	M	S.D.	M	S.D.
Pekings	(N = 21)		(N = 20)		(N = 38)		(N = 33)		(N = 20)		(N = 74)		(N = 0)		(N = 25)	
Percent followed	90		60		92		70		90		51		...		44	
Ave. latency (sec.)	361.3	274.3	382.6	212.3	261.3	243.6	452.2	238.8	198.3	184.7	275.0	271.3	...		341.6	217.5
Ave. duration (sec.)	531.5	364.7	455.1	215.1	668.7	551.2	524.7	328.9	640.6	231.9	661.8	400.9	...		604.8	274.0
Mallards	(N = 20)		(N = 20)		(N = 16)		(N = 29)		(N = 18)		(N = 16)		(N = 20)		(N = 20)	
Percent followed	95		60		63		59		83		69		100		50	
Ave. latency (sec.)	265.3	206.2	342.7	241.6	274.7	252.8	493.4	268.2	323.7	265.3	173.7	141.3	321.1	274.8	474.0	365.6
Ave. duration (sec.)	440.8	315.4	513.5	307.0	576.9	254.2	301.3	244.2	434.7	324.0	761.4	380.8	603.1	309.2	212.2	317.5

TABLE 19
Statistical Analysis of Pekings' and Mallards' Following-Response to Various Audiovisual Combinations

Species	Calls and Replicas	p Value (2-tailed)
	Incidence of Response (proportion responded)	
Peking	wood duck/ ♀ peking vs. wood duck/ ♂ mallard decoy	ns
Peking	wood duck/ ♀ peking vs. wood duck/ ♀ wood duck	.10
Peking	mallard/ ♀ mallard vs. wood duck/ ♀ mallard	.06
Peking	mallard/ ♀ peking vs. wood duck/ ♀ peking	.04
Peking	mallard/ ♂ mallard decoy vs. wood duck/ ♂ mallard decoy	.006
Peking	wood duck/ ♀ mallard vs. wood duck/ ♀ wood duck	ns
Mallard	mallard/ ♀ mallard vs. mallard/ ♀ peking	.04
Mallard	mallard/ ♀ peking vs. mallard/ ♂ mallard decoy	ns
Mallard	mallard/ ♀ mallard vs. wood duck/ ♀ mallard	.02
Mallard	wood duck/ ♂ mallard decoy vs. wood duck/ ♀ wood duck	ns
Mallard	mallard/ ♀ peking vs. mallard/ ♀ wood duck	.01
Mallard	mallard/ ♀ wood duck vs. wood duck/ ♀ wood duck	.001
Mallard	mallard/ ♂ mallard decoy vs. wood duck/ ♂ mallard decoy	ns
Mallard	mallard/ ♂ mallard decoy vs. mallard/ ♀ wood duck	ns
Peking and mallard	wood duck/ ♂ mallard decoy	ns
Peking and mallard	mallard/ ♀ peking	.02
	Latency of Response (responders only)	
Peking	mallard/ ♀ mallard vs. mallard/ ♀ peking	.08
Peking	wood duck/ ♀ mallard vs. wood duck/ ♀ peking	ns
Peking	mallard/ ♀ mallard vs. wood duck/ ♀ mallard	ns
Peking	mallard/ ♀ peking vs. wood duck/ ♀ peking	.002

(Table 19 continued)

Species	Calls and Replicas	p Value (2-tailed)
Peking	mallard/ ♂ mallard decoy vs. wood duck/ ♂ mallard decoy	ns
Peking	wood duck/ ♂ peking vs. wood duck/ ♀ wood duck	ns
Peking	wood duck/ ♂ mallard decoy vs. wood duck/ ♀ wood duck	.02
Peking	mallard/ ♂ mallard decoy vs. mallard/ ♀ mallard	ns
Peking	mallard/ ♂ mallard decoy vs. mallard/ ♀ peking	.08
Mallard	wood duck/ ♀ mallard vs. wood duck/ ♂ mallard decoy	.001
Mallard	wood duck/ ♂ peking vs. wood duck/ ♂ mallard decoy	ns
Mallard	mallard/ ♀ wood duck vs. wood duck/ ♀ wood duck	ns
Mallard	mallard/ ♀ mallard vs. mallard/ ♀ wood duck	.10
Mallard	wood duck/ ♂ mallard decoy vs. wood duck/ ♀ wood duck	ns
Mallard	wood duck/ ♀ mallard vs. wood duck/ ♀ wood duck	ns
Mallard	mallard/ ♀ mallard vs. wood duck/ ♀ mallard	ns
Mallard	mallard/ ♂ peking vs. wood duck/ ♀ peking	.04
Mallard	mallard/ ♂ mallard decoy vs. wood duck/ ♂ mallard decoy	ns
Mallard	wood duck/ ♀ mallard vs. wood duck/ ♀ peking	.06
Peking and mallard	mallard/ ♂ mallard decoy	ns
Peking and mallard	wood duck/ ♂ mallard decoy	ns
Peking and mallard	mallard/ ♀ mallard	ns
Peking and mallard	wood duck/ ♀ wood duck	ns
Peking and mallard	mallard/ ♀ peking	ns

Duration of Response
(responders only)

Species	Calls and Replicas	p Value (2-tailed)
Peking	mallard/ ♀ mallard vs. mallard/ ♀ peking	ns
Peking	wood duck/ ♀ mallard vs. wood duck/ ♀ peking	ns
Peking	wood duck/ ♀ peking vs. wood duck/ ♂ mallard decoy	.06
Peking	wood duck/ ♀ mallard vs. wood duck/ ♂ mallard decoy	.06

(Table 19 continued)

Species	Calls and Replicas	p Value (2-tailed)
Peking	wood duck/ ♀ peking vs. wood duck/ ♀ wood duck	ns
Peking	wood duck/ ♀ mallard vs. wood duck/ ♀ wood duck	ns
Peking	mallard/ ♀ mallard vs. mallard/ ♂ mallard decoy	ns
Peking	wood duck/ ♀ mallard decoy vs. wood duck/ ♀ wood duck	ns
Peking	mallard/ ♀ mallard vs. wood duck/ ♀ mallard	ns
Peking	mallard/ ♀ peking vs. wood duck/ ♀ peking	.04
Peking	mallard/ ♀ peking vs. wood duck/ ♀ peking	.01
Mallard	wood duck/ ♀ mallard vs. wood duck/ ♀ peking	.04
Mallard	mallard/ ♀ mallard vs. mallard/ ♀ peking	ns
Mallard	mallard/ ♀ mallard vs. mallard/ ♀ wood duck	ns
Mallard	mallard/ ♂ mallard decoy vs. mallard/ ♀ wood duck	ns
Mallard	mallard/ ♀ mallard vs. wood duck/ ♀ mallard	ns
Mallard	mallard/ ♂ mallard decoy vs. wood duck/ ♂ mallard decoy	.02
Mallard	wood duck/ ♂ mallard decoy vs. wood duck/ ♀ wood duck	.04
Mallard	wood duck/ ♀ peking vs. wood duck/ ♂ mallard decoy	.006
Mallard	wood duck/ ♀ mallard vs. wood duck/ ♂ mallard decoy	.08
Mallard	mallard/ ♀ wood duck vs. wood duck/ ♀ wood duck	.004
Mallard	wood duck/ ♀ mallard vs. wood duck/ ♀ wood duck	.02
Peking and mallard	wood duck/ ♀ wood duck	.01
Peking and mallard	mallard/ ♀ mallard	ns
Peking and mallard	mallard/ ♂ mallard decoy	.04
Peking and mallard	wood duck/ ♂ mallard decoy	ns
Peking and mallard	mallard/ ♀ peking	ns
Peking and mallard	wood duck/ ♀ peking	.04

NOTE: See table 18. ns = two-tailed $p > .10$.

mine the statistical reliability of almost any outcome shown in table 18.)

Discussion

In answer to the main question, the more nearly natural maternal audiovisual configurations, while quite effective, were not unique in their effectiveness in promoting the following-response of either the peking or the mallard ducklings. While the presence of the mallard maternal call plays a crucial role in elevating the birds' response (percent followed) to the various visual replicas, peculiarities in the visual composition of the stimulus configuration (interacting with the call) significantly influence the latency and duration of the birds' response. In this respect, each audiovisual object is a somewhat unique perceptual configuration, so that a knowledge of the independent effectiveness of the auditory and visual components does not allow one to predict the relative strength of the ducklings' response when the components are brought together as a unit (i.e., the effect on the ducklings' response is not strictly additive in an arithmetic sense). For example, among all of the visual replicas, the pekings gave their weakest visual response to the peking hen (chapter 6). When the mallard call was brought into conjunction with each of the replicas, the pekings responded as strongly (or even more strongly) to the peking hen as they did to the mallard and wood duck hens. Perhaps an even more striking example of this phenomenon was the mallards' tremendous response (latency and duration) to the wood duck call emanating from the male mallard decoy; in the purely visual test (chapter 6), the mallards were absolutely unresponsive to the male mallard decoy.[1]

1. It is possible to question the foregoing interpretation by asking whether the differences in response to the various audiovisual configurations, although they are statistically reliable, might not be attributable to sampling error or "batch differences." The sample sizes in some cases were rather small and the individual variation was, as usual, enormous. Based on the fact that the particular trends

SEVEN

In previously published work (Gottlieb 1965a and 1966), it has been shown that the species' maternal call is the decisive factor in determining which of two similar visual replicas will be approached or followed in a simultaneous audiovisual choice test (two different maternal calls emanating from two similar replicas). Consequently, we have not broadened the present results any further in that direction. A useful approach, which we have not fully exploited, concerns the ducklings' visual preference in a simultaneous audiovisual choice test in which the mallard maternal call emanates from two different replicas. In this way it would be possible to specify exactly the importance of the visual attributes of the mallard hen in comparison to the wood duck hen or the male mallard decoy, and so on. We have completed only one such experiment; and, though the results are instructive, it is not the most relevant test which could have been performed. (A long-term breakdown in our mobile, audiovisual test equipment forced us to cancel other tests.)

At 21 to 31 hours after hatching, 19 mallard ducklings were exposed to the mallard maternal call emanating from both the mallard hen and the peking hen in a simultaneous audiovisual choice test (20-minute following test). Sixteen

reported above have been observed from one season to another, I am inclined to place confidence in the general reliability of the findings with the peking and mallard ducklings. The unknown and uncontrolled variables which affect the repeatability of work on domestic chicks is quite another matter, however; and it has been a serious problem in this laboratory as well as other laboratories. (See, for example, n. 5, p. 7 of Hamburger *et al.* 1965.) Because of their unreliability, we have discontinued using chicks or chick embryos for anything other than preliminary work. If one plans a sustained research program, it is risky to use chicks as the main or sole experimental animal unless the behavior of control groups is constantly reexamined and very large Ns are employed. The difficulty is not obviated when the eggs are obtained from a single supplier. As far as we know, the results of the tests conducted with chicks which are presented in this monograph are repeatable and are not restricted to the white rock variety — e.g., white leghorns can discriminate the chicken maternal call in simultaneous auditory choice tests (Oppenheim, Jones, and Gottlieb 1970).

TABLE 20

Simultaneous Audiovisual Choice Test: Mallard Ducklings' Response to Mallard Maternal Call Emanating From Stuffed Mallard Hen and Stuffed Peking Hen during Twenty-Minute Following Test

	♀ Mallard	*p* value (2-tailed)	♀ Peking
Preference	69%	.03	25%
Ave. latency (sec.)	470.5	*ns*	677.4
S.D.	432.4		552.8
Ave. duration (sec.)	468.5	.04	220.8
S.D.	447.6		365.5

NOTE: The preference percent totals less than 100 because one bird which responded did not show a preference for either replica; that bird's score is included in the latency and duration figures, however.

ns = two-tailed $p > .10$.

(84%) of the birds responded and, as shown in table 20, they showed a reliable preference for the mallard call/mallard hen audiovisual combination.

Because other tests were not performed, it is not possible to make any general conclusions about the birds' sensitivity to the appropriate audiovisual configuration in contexts other than the one above. It is obvious from the results, however, that this is the best procedure for settling the question of the duckling's ability to perceive and discriminate appropriate from nonappropriate maternal audiovisual configurations, and to get a firm conclusion on the significance of the visual component when the proper auditory component is present.

Summary

The normal or natural maternal audiovisual combination is not uniquely effective in eliciting the following-response of peking and mallard ducklings.

Although every audiovisual combination provokes a stronger following-response than either component alone, a knowledge of the independent effectiveness of each component does not allow one exactly to predict the relative

SEVEN

strength of the ducklings' following-response when the two components are brought together as a unit.

The most powerful test for determining the ducklings' sensitivity to the proper visual component of the audiovisual combination is one in which the appropriate maternal call emanates from two different replicas in a simultaneous choice test.

8

Prenatal Ontogeny of the Duckling's Capability to Respond Selectively to the Maternal Call of Its Species

WITH the previous experiments as a background, the present chapter describes the initial step in our analysis of the prenatal ontogeny of the birds' capability to respond selectively to the appropriate maternal call in the absence of prior exposure to same. As has been shown in this monograph, and in previously published experiments (e.g., Gottlieb 1965a and 1966), the maternal call is the primary basis on which the young birds are able to discriminate a parent of their own species from a parent of another species. The important ontogenetic questions are: how early does this capability develop, and what are the factors responsible for its initial development and final perfection? The present experiments deal with the first question, and the succeeding chapters deal with the second question.

In a previous report (Gottlieb 1968b) it was shown that, on the day before hatching (Day 26–27), peking duck embryos are able to make a discriminative response to the mallard maternal call when exposed to the mallard call, wood duck maternal call, chicken maternal call, and duckling (sib) call. The behavioral sign of the discrimination was a statistically reliable increase in baseline rate of oral activity (bill-clapping) when the embryos were exposed to the mallard maternal call. The embryos showed no change in their baseline rate of oral activity when they were exposed to any of the other maternal calls or the sib call. On the physiological side, the embryos showed a reliable increase in heart rate to all of the calls. Thus, behavioral activation (specifically, rate of bill-clapping) was in evidence upon exposure to the species' maternal call and absent upon exposure to the other calls — physiological activation (increase in heart rate) occurred upon exposure to all the calls; thus this latter measure can not be used as a sign of selective responsiveness at the later stages of embryonic development.

It remains to examine the embryo's behavioral and physiological reactivity to the maternal calls at earlier stages of development to ascertain the lower age limit of the selective response to the maternal call under normal conditions of incubation. It should be borne in mind that in the present experiments, except where otherwise indicated, the embryos were communally incubated and had heard their own vocalizations and those of sibs prior to testing. In this way the typical developmental course of the embryo's selective auditory response could be charted under circumstances of normally occurring stimulation. In the experiments described in the succeeding chapters, the normal situation has been manipulated to determine the contribution of such stimulation to the typical course of species-specific auditory perceptual development.

So the reader may better appreciate the procedure used to study the embryo's behavior during the final week of incubation, a synopsis of the embryo's positional relationship to the air space follows. The peking duck embryo usually hatches early on Day 27. On Day 26–27, the bill of all normally positioned embryos is in the air space at the large end of the egg, and the action of the bill has pipped the shell over the air space. On Day 25 the bills of most embryos are well into the air space and some embryos may have pipped the shell. On Day 24 about one-half of the embryos have begun to penetrate into the air space, and none have pipped the shell. In the usual course of events, it is at this time (Day 24) that pulmonary respiration is fairly well established and the embryos can vocalize. Vocalizations are usually feeble and infrequent early on Day 24, and the ability to vocalize is positively correlated with penetration into the air space. There is great variability in the actual time the embryos first penetrate the air space and, thus, in the onset of vocal ability. On Day 23, none of the embryos are in the air space. The bills of some embryos may have begun to work toward the air space and create a tent-like protrusion in the chorioallantois and inner shell membrane. A small proportion of embryos can vocalize as early as Day 23, prior to actual penetration into the air space. If the embryos are prematurely (artificially) brought into the air space late on Day 23, all of them are capable of vocalizing about 30 minutes after they have been exposed to air (Gottlieb and Vandenbergh 1968, p. 309, table 2). On Day 22 the bill of the embryo has not yet risen to the tenting stage.

Method

Apparatus
As shown in figure 9, a modified human infant incubator with armholes was used so the eggs could be opened at the proper temperature and humidity inside the incubator, and the embryos could be observed through the transparent walls during the experiment. Ink-writing pens driven by a Grass Model III EEG (polygraph) machine recorded oral activity (bill-clapping), heart beat (EKG), and vocalization. To obtain the record of heart rate, three Grass #E-2 fine platinum needle electrodes were inserted under the skin on various parts of the embryo's body, and to determine rate of bill-

FIG. 9. Prenatal test apparatus. The egg is kept at proper temperature and humidity inside the transparent incubator. Electrodes have been affixed to the embryo inside the egg (see fig. 10) and the polygraph machine (right) records bill-clapping, vocalization (via microphone above egg), and heart beat. The observer also monitors the vocalizations with earphones.

clapping one electrode was placed in the lower mandible (see figures 10 and 11). Heart beat was recorded on one channel of the polygraph, and bill-clapping was recorded on another channel. A microphone, positioned about one inch from the embryo's bill, was connected through an audio amplifier to the EEG machine. The embryo's vocalizations thus caused pen deflections on one channel of the polygraph, thereby providing a record of rate of vocalization. (In practice it proved to be equally reliable for the observer to simply count the vocalizations by ear: earphones attached to the audio amplifier permitted all sounds to be continuously monitored.) A Nagra III tape recorder was used to play the calls. All the equipment was located in a sound-attenuated room. Inside the incubator, the background noise level was 47–50 dB with the paper drive of the polygraph in operation.

Operative Technique
One of two variations of the same technique was employed to gain access to the embryo, depending on its age. The two technical variations are shown in figures 10 and 11. The main difference was that Day 25–27 embryos were left in their normal position. In embryos younger than Day 25, it was necessary to pull their head out of the shell to insert the electrodes. The general procedure was as follows: First, the egg was candled and the air space traced in pencil on the egg. Next, the egg was rubbed with cotton soaked in 70% alcohol and placed on towels inside the incubator. With the point of a scissors, a hole was pierced in the shell over the air space and the shell and outer shell membrane removed (figure 10-*1*). A few drops of warm saline solution were dropped on the inner shell membrane to render the chorioallantoic (CA) blood vessels and the embryo visible (figure 10-*2*). The inner shell membrane and CA were cut, avoiding the large CA blood vessels, and gently pushed away from the Day 25–27 embryos (figure 11-*?*). For recording EKG in the Day 25–27 embryos, a narrow strip was also cut in the shell to partially expose the back of the bird (figures 11-*2* and 11-*3*). In younger embryos some of the fluids were drained to better determine the embryo's position. Between Day 20 to Day 24 the embryo is positioned at the large end of the egg with its head curled clockwise beneath its right wing (this is the normal embryonic position during late incubation). Under these conditions, the back, neck, and the wing are usually visible. The bill or neck is grasped with small forceps, and the head or neck is gently and slowly pulled or pried out of the shell (figures 10-*3* and 10-*4*).

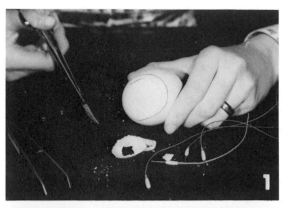

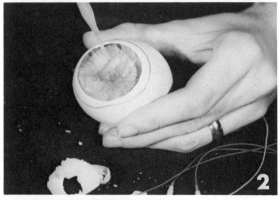

100

WAYNE J. ARENDT

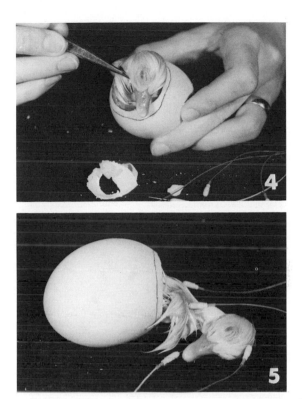

FIG. 10. Procedure for recording from the peking duck embryo during Days 20 to 24 of development. (*1*) The shell over the air space is removed. (*2*) Warm saline is applied to inner shell membrane in order to render the chorioallantoic blood vessels and embryo visible. (*3*) Curved forceps is placed under the neck of the embryo, and (*4*) the embryo's head is slowly pulled out of the egg. (Before the forceps is used, a slit is made in the chorioallantois and the membrane is gently pushed to the side.) (*5*) One electrode is inserted into the lower mandible to record the movement artifact associated with bill-clapping; to record heart beat, an electrode is inserted sub-dermally near the heart, the ground electrode is placed under the skin on the embryo's head, and the indifferent electrode is inserted in the skin on the embryo's back.

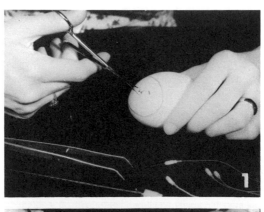

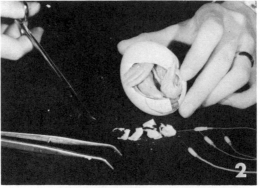

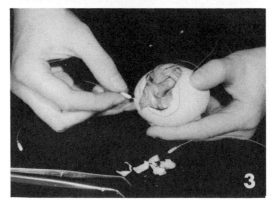

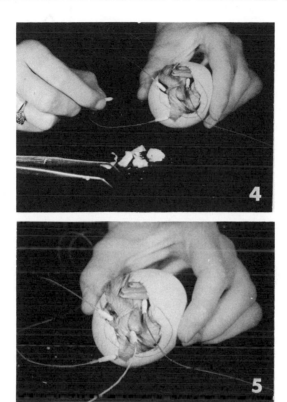

FIG. 11. Procedure for recording from peking duck embryo during Days 25 to 27 of development. (*1*) The shell is cut away beginning in the vicinity of the embryo's bill (the egg is pipped or very close to pipping at this stage). (*2*) Shell is removed revealing embryo's bill, foot, and wing. Strip of shell is removed (bottom of egg as shown) over embryo's back for indifferent electrode. (*3*) Indifferent electrode is placed beneath skin on embryo's back. Note that the embryo is not pulled out of the egg at this stage; the embryo retains its normal position during recording. (*4*) The heart electrode and ground electrode have been inserted as in figure 10, and the bill-clapping electrode is about to be inserted into lower mandible. (*5*) Embryo is prepared for recording of heart beat and bill-clapping.

Embryos which were not properly positioned at the large end of the egg were discarded.

For recording oral activity, an electrode was inserted in the lower mandible. (Inserting the electrode in the loose skin beneath the lower mandible gives similar results on rate-per-min. of bill-clapping.) Displacements of the bill cause movement artifacts on the polygraphic record, and these were used to measure rate of oral activity (see figure 12). A ground electrode was placed beneath the loose skin on the top of the head. The electrodes were plugged into an electrode board located inside the incubator. The gain control on the polygraph was adjusted so that the pen deflections were well defined.

For EKG recordings the active electrode was inserted under the right wing. A second (indifferent) electrode was placed under the loose skin in the bird's back. With a ground selector, the electrode on the bird's head served as a ground for both oral activity and EKG recordings.

After all the electrodes had been inserted, the embryo was oriented so that its bill was about one inch from the microphone. Figure 12 shows the actual wave forms for vocalization, heart beat, and bill-clapping as they appeared on the polygraphic record.

Testing Procedure

After an acclimation period of 15 to 30 minutes, the baseline recordings of bill-clapping, vocalization, and heart rate were obtained during a 5-minute prestimulation period. During this period and the following two periods (stimulation and poststimulation periods), the observer watched the embryo and monitored the embryo's vocalizations with the aid of earphones. All sounds and gross movement were marked and identified on the recordings. At the end of the 5-minute baseline period, one of the calls was played on the tape recorder. The calls lasted approximately 25 seconds during which time the call repeated itself 7 times. A period of 30 seconds from the beginning of the first burst of the call was used for measuring activity during the stimulation period. Each embryo was exposed to only one call (i.e., 7 bursts of one call). These were the same calls to which the hatchlings were exposed in the previous postnatal experiments. The embryo's activity was similarly monitored during a 5-minute

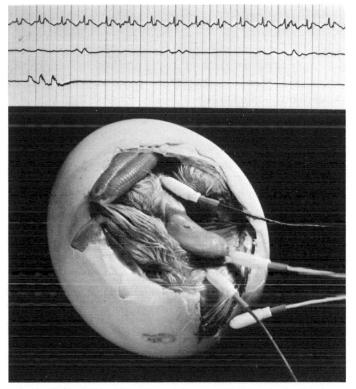

FIG. 12. Peking duck embryo (Day 25–27) with recording electrodes in place. Top line shows heart beat, middle line depicts bill-clapping, and bottom line shows occurrence of three vocalizations (recorded via microphone above embryo as shown in fig. 9). (From fig. 7, Gottlieb, *Quart. Rev. Biol.* 43 (1968): 168. Reproduced by courtesy of the publisher.)

poststimulation period. Inside the incubator, where the embryo was placed, the intensity of all the calls was in the range of 55–66 db SPL (Brüel & Kjaer Precision Sound Level Meter Type 2203 with directional microphone; readings taken on Scale B, fast, with setting on 60 dB).

Statistical Evaluation
To evaluate the statistical reliability of changes during the stimulation period, the Wilcoxon Matched-Pairs Signed-Ranks Test was employed. This nonparametric test compares each embryo's performance in the stimulation period with its performance in the prestimulation period, specifically taking into account direction of change and magnitude of change. If the direction of change is consistent for all the embryos in the group, then the magnitude of change can be small and still achieve statistical reliability. If only a majority of embryos share a certain direction of change, then, to achieve reliability, the magnitude of the majority's change must be large, and the magnitude of change in the minority's performance must be relatively small. Since there is a great deal of individual variation in baseline rates, the Wilcoxon test seems particularly appropriate in the present context. While, for convenience of presentation, mean values and standard deviations are shown in the following tables, it should be noted that the calculation of the Wilcoxon test does not involve group averages or standard deviations.

Results
On Day 26–27, the embryo shows an activation of bill-clapping which is specific to the maternal call of its species (mallard). As indicated by the previously published data (Gottlieb 1968b) in table 21, the embryo's heart rate increases upon exposure to any of the maternal or sibling calls. An increase in the embryo's vocalization rate occurs only in response to the mallard maternal call and the sibling brooding-like call. Since the increase in rate of bill-clapping

TABLE 21

Evidence of Auditory Discrimination in Duck Embryos (Day 26–27): Rate per Minute of Bill-clapping, Vocalization, and Heart Beat before, during, and after Thirty-Second Exposure to Various Calls

Calls	Bill-Clapping		Vocalization		Heart Rate	
	M	S.D.	M	S.D.	M	S.D.
Mallard ($N = 20$)						
Before	32.8	18.4	2.6	2.2	217.8	24.3
During	53.3[b]	24.7	24.0[b]	25.1	243.8[b]	34.0
After	32.0	25.2	4.0	5.5	227.8	29.1
Duckling, sib ($N = 20$)						
Before	34.8	44.7	4.0	4.7	212.0	33.4
During	45.9	73.6	7.6[a]	7.4	227.9[b]	38.4
After	30.8	31.8	3.5	4.1	216.1	35.8
Wood duck ($N = 20$)						
Before	39.2	30.4	2.5	2.8	236.9	34.2
During	39.6	41.1	4.8	7.1	245.0[a]	30.7
After	31.9	22.0	2.3	1.7	237.6	33.3
Chicken ($N = 20$)						
Before	19.4	12.9	3.0	4.7	215.9	32.3
During	20.6	17.8	9.4	13.3	238.3[b]	37.6
After	19.3	13.1	2.1	2.8	211.1	27.7

NOTE: Statistical reliability of change from baseline rate of activity is denoted by two-tailed p values: [a] $= p < .05$; [b] $= p < .005$.

occurs only to the mallard call, that measure can be used as the behavioral sign of a discriminative response on the part of the embryo to the maternal call of its own species.

Since the increase in bill-clapping to the mallard call may simply be one aspect of a more general behavioral activation, the response of other embryos with electrodes in their legs was examined on Day 26–27. One group was exposed to the mallard maternal call, and the other group was played the wood duck maternal call. As shown in table 22, the embryos which were exposed to the mallard call showed a reliable increase in rate of leg movement, while the embryos exposed to the wood duck call did not show such a change.

TABLE 22
Rate per Minute of Leg Movement in Duck Embryos
Tested with the Mallard and Wood Duck Maternal
Calls on Day 26

Calls	M	S.D.
Mallard ($N = 19$)		
Before	11.8	13.3
During	23.3	21.7
After	13.1	13.2
Wood duck ($N = 14$)		
Before	26.6	43.9
During	29.0	41.5
After	24.6	35.5

NOTE: The increase in rate of leg movement in response to the mallard call was statistically reliable ($p<.001$), whereas the change to the wood duck call was not reliable ($p>.10$). As is the case with the other experiments in this chapter, each embryo was exposed to only one of the calls (i.e., the groups are always independent). There is great variability in baseline rates of embryonic activity depending on electrode placement, specific stage in relation to hatching, and so on, so all baseline values should be regarded as relative. Whether or not the embryos (as a group) *change* their baseline rate of activity upon stimulation has thus far been shown to be reliable, despite the value of the baseline level.

Thus, it may be concluded that the embryo's behavioral response to the mallard call is of a general character on Day 26–27 and is not restricted to bill movements. The other maternal calls simply do not behaviorally activate the embryo, though they do cause a change in heart rate on Day 26–27.

To determine the onset of the embryo's discriminative response to the mallard call, embryos were exposed to the mallard call, sib call, and wood duck call on Day 25 through Day 20. A different group of embryos was used on each day and for each call. As shown in table 23, the embryos showed a reliable increase in bill-clapping to the mallard call on Days 25 and 24, a reliable decrease in bill-clapping to the mallard call on Days 23 and 22, and no overt change on Days 21 and 20. It is worthy of note that the age at which

TABLE 23

Species-Specific Auditory Discrimination in Communally Incubated Duck Embryos during the Final Quarter of Embryological Development: Rate per Minute of Bill-Clapping, Vocalization, and Heart Beat before, during, and after Thirty-Second Exposure to Mallard, Sib, and Wood Duck Calls

	Bill-Clapping		Vocalization		Heart Rate	
	M	S.D.	M	S.D.	M	S.D.
Mallard Call						
Day 25 (N = 19)						
Before	67.8	41.6	1.8	2.8	219.1	25.7
During	127.8[c]	95.9	15.7[c]	13.3	217.3	20.4
After	91.7	60.3	2.5	3.1	211.4	20.2
Day 24 (N = 20)						
Before	38.4	27.5	0.8	2.0	187.9	24.6
During	61.6[b]	44.0	5.7[a]	11.0	189.8	23.9
After	47.0	24.1	0.9	1.7	186.5	22.7
Day 23 (N = 25)						
Before	36.9	27.6	. . .	. . .	188.6	23.8
During	19.7[c]	26.3	. . .	. . .	189.4	23.6
After	37.9	29.5	. . .	. . .	190.9	23.8
Day 22 (N = 20)						
Before	25.4	21.6	. . .	. . .	193.5	23.0
During	13.9[b]	23.2	. . .	. . .	194.8	24.4
After	23.6	16.7	. . .	. . .	193.2	22.1
Day 21 (N = 20)						
Before	63.7	43.1	. . .	. . .	207.0	27.5
During	48.9	48.4	. . .	. . .	207.6	27.0
After	66.6	34.1	. . .	. . .	208.1	27.4
Day 20 (N = 20)						
Before	49.0	39.7	. . .	. . .	221.1	24.4
During	75.0	114.2	. . .	. . .	221.4	24.3
After	74.0	47.5	. . .	. . .	222.0	24.4
Sib Call						
Day 24 (N = 20)						
Before	84.1	66.9	0.5	1.0	184.5	23.3
During	79.4	89.2	0.5	2.2	188.0	24.9
After	72.5	35.0	0.9	1.5	185.7	25.8

(Table 23 continued)

| | Bill-Clapping | | Vocalization | | Heart Rate | |
	M	S.D.	M	S.D.	M	S.D.
			Wood Duck Call			
Day 24 (*N* = 20)						
Before	66.8	39.8	0.5	0.7	211.3	23.7
During	65.4	65.1	0.2	0.9	212.4	22.2
After	73.2	41.8	0.3	0.4	213.0	22.6
Day 23 (*N* = 20)						
Before	23.5	15.6	. . .	. . .	182.1	19.4
During	24.8	32.0	. . .	. . .	184.2	20.6
After	23.8	22.5	. . .	. . .	184.2	20.8

NOTE: Vocalization is rare or nonexistent prior to Day 24, so that measure is not used with the younger embryos. Statistical reliability of change from baseline rate of activity is denoted by two-tailed *p* values: [a] $= p < .05$; [b] $= p < .01$; [c] $= p < .005$.

the mallard call begins to provoke an overt excitatory change in bill-clapping corresponds to the time when the embryos have moved into the air space and are breathing; before that time the mallard call inhibits the ongoing rate of bill-clapping. While the changes (increase or decrease) in bill-clapping are reliable, the accompanying heart rate change is of borderline reliability or unreliable on all days prior to Day 26. It is particularly interesting that on Day 22 the heart rate tends to increase to the mallard call (two-tailed $p = .10$), while the rate of bill-clapping is reliably decreased. (The occurrence of vocalizations in embryos younger than Day 24 is very infrequent, therefore this measure is not reported in the youngest embryos.)

As can be further seen in table 23, in contrast to the mallard maternal call, the wood duck maternal call does not provoke any behavioral change on Day 24 (when the mallard call activates bill-clapping) or on Day 23 (when the mallard call deactivates bill-clapping). Similarly, the sib call does not cause any change in bill-clapping rate on Day 24. Thus, within this limited context, the communally incubated duck embryo's behavioral response to the mallard call is a discriminative one on all days tested.

The next question is whether the duck embryo's response to the mallard call is a discriminative response from the start (i.e., on Day 22), or whether the discrimination develops gradually. The previously mentioned embryos were communally incubated under conditions where they were exposed to the vocalizations of more advanced embryos as well as their own vocalizations (in the case of Day 24 or older embryos). The next experiment was addressed to the question of whether the Day 22 embryos, the youngest ones to give an overt behavioral response to the mallard call, are able to give a discriminative response to the mallard call in the absence of prior exposure to the vocalizations of advanced sibs. The Day 22 embryos do not vocalize, so to answer this question it was necessary only to keep the eggs segregated from more advanced embryos. This was accomplished by incubating the eggs in a separate sound-treated room. On Day 22 these embryos were then exposed to the mallard call, the sib call, the wood duck call, or the chicken call. As shown in table 24, the embryos are capable of making a discriminative response to the mallard call at the outset — specifically, the Day 22 embryos showed a reliable decrease in bill-clapping to the mallard call and no change in their ongoing rate of bill-clapping when exposed to the duckling (sib) call, the wood duck call, or the chicken call. Each embryo was exposed to only one of the calls.

Discussion

The present experiments indicated that the duck embryo's behavioral response to the mallard maternal call goes through three stages under normal conditions of communal incubation: on Days 20 and 21 they were overtly unresponsive to the mallard call; on Days 22 and 23 they showed an inhibition (decrease) in their bill-clapping rate; and on Days 24 to 27 they showed an increase in their rate of bill-clapping

TABLE 24
Evidence of Auditory Discrimination in Duck Embryos (Day 22):
Rate per Minute of Bill-Clapping and Heart Beat before, during,
and after Thirty-Second Exposure to Various Calls

Calls	Bill-Clapping		Heart Rate	
	M	S.D.	M	S.D.
Mallard (N = 30)				
Before	58.7	26.1	194.9	25.5
During	48.7[a]	97.9	194.4	25.1
After	64.4	42.4	194.1	26.5
Duckling (N = 22)				
Before	59.6	32.2	188.0	17.8
During	59.6	53.8	189.2	17.0
After	47.1	26.7	190.8	16.6
Wood duck (N = 31)				
Before	34.2	25.6	186.3	19.1
During	44.6	67.0	185.9	20.3
After	43.7	34.5	184.8	20.3
Chicken (N = 31)				
Before	43.2	26.0	190.0	21.6
During	51.7	77.5	189.0	21.1
After	49.4	33.5	189.3	20.3

NOTE: Statistical reliability of change from baseline rate of activity is designated
by two-tailed p value: [a] = $p < .05$. None of the Day-22 embryos vocalized during
the test; hence, that measure is not utilized in this age group.

when exposed to the mallard call. The changeover from an
inhibitory to an excitatory effect coincides with the embryo's
penetration into the air space, the establishment of pulmonary respiration, and, consequently, the embryo's ability
to vocalize. At all ages tested the embryos were behaviorally
unresponsive to the maternal calls of other species; thus, the
embryos' behavioral response to the mallard call is a discriminative reaction, and it occurs as early as Day 22 (five
days before hatching). While the embryos do not show an
increase in bill-clapping to the sib call, on Day 26 they do
show an increase in vocalization rate when exposed to the
sib call.

DUCK EMBRYO'S RESPONSE TO MATERNAL CALL

Bill-clapping is a convenient and reliable quantitative measure of the embryo's response to auditory stimulation (and to visual stimulation [Oppenheim 1968]). The change in rate of bill-clapping, however, reflects a more general bodily response to the stimulation provided by the mallard call; embryos tested on Day 26 also showed a selective increase in rate of leg movement in response to the mallard call as opposed to the wood duck call. Since coordinated leg and head movements are involved in hatching (Hamburger and Oppenheim 1967), it would be of interest to determine if exposure to the mallard call would affect the time of hatching. In nature the mallard hen begins to vocalize as the first embryos hatch, so it is possible that such stimulation may have a "synchronizing effect" by accelerating the time of hatching in those embryos which are lagging behind in hatching. While all of this is quite speculative, it should be noted that, if true, this apparently would be a different synchronizing mechanism than that shown by Vince's quail embryos (1968). Her work suggests that the "clicking" produced by the embryos themselves regulates the time of hatching in those species. Since quail are said to leave the nest within a relatively few hours after hatching, and ducks (Gottlieb 1965b) stay in the nest for a longer period, a synchronizing mechanism would be of greater import (and probably more exacting) in quail than in duck species.

Finally, the present experiments indicated that the duck embryo's ability to selectively respond to its maternal call precedes its ability[1] to vocalize and is not dependent on hearing the vocalizations of more advanced embryos.

The next experiments examine whether such stimulation plays any role in regulating the embryo's subsequent re-

1. The embryo has the ability to vocalize earlier than Day 24 if it is prematurely and artificially brought into the air space (Gottlieb and Vandenbergh 1968). Under normal conditions this ability usually does not manifest itself until the embryo begins to penetrate into the air space (Day 24–25).

sponsiveness to the mallard call or in bringing the hatchling's discriminative ability to final perfection.

Summary
The peking duck embryo becomes overtly responsive to the maternal call of its species on Day 22 (five days before hatching). At that time it is already able to selectively respond to the appropriate maternal call, and this initial capability is not dependent on prior exposure to its own vocalizations or those of sibs.

9

The Influence of Normally Occurring Stimulation on the Duck Embryo's Response to the Maternal Call of Its Species

THE duck embryo is able to respond selectively to the maternal call of its species on Day 22 (five days before hatching) in the absence of any previous auditory stimulation from itself, sibs, or the parent. At this time the embryo shows an inhibition of bill-clapping (—) upon exposure to the call, and on Day 23 it also shows the same response (—) Beginning on Day 24, the embryo displays an increased rate of bill-clapping (+) to the maternal call, a pattern of response (+) which continues to Day 27 (hatching). Since the embryos begin to vocalize on Day 24, it is of interest to ask whether this sort of normally occurring stimulation plays any role in regulating the developmental sequence of the embryo's response to the maternal call. In essence we are asking whether the embryo's response to the maternal call goes through a series of predetermined stages or whether the specific kind of response which the embryo makes is probabilistic, in the sense that it is determined by the amount of auditory stimulation which the embryo normally encounters.

To examine the above question, two experiments were

NINE

performed: the first experiment involved placing the embryos in individual auditory isolation on Day 23 and testing the embryos' response to the mallard call on Day 24. Since isolation reduces the total amount of auditory stimulation (i.e., a limited amount of self-stimulation can still occur), the question is whether the embryos will show the usual increase in bill-clapping to the mallard call on Day 24. The other experiment involved an attempt to accelerate the appearance of the increase in bill-clapping — to determine if the increase would appear on Day 23 instead of Day 24 if the embryos were prematurely exposed to sib calls on Days 21 and 22.

Method

All the isolated embryos were incubated in a sound-attenuated room where no other advanced embryos or hatchlings were present. At the end of Day 22 each embryo in the isolation group was placed in an individual sound-attenuated compartment of a specially built incubator (shown in figures 13 and 14) in a sound-treated room. Although these compartments were not absolutely soundproof, the usual vocalizations of Day-24 embryos would not penetrate between compartments. The individual embryos could, of course, hear their own self-produced vocalizations, so the present condition represents only partial auditory deprivation in any event. It is our impression that isolated embryos vocalize less than communally incubated embryos, but we have not validated that impression by objective recording. A total of 38 embryos was involved in this experiment — 21 were tested to the mallard call on the first half of Day 24, and 17 were tested on the last half of Day 24.

The embryos which received augmented exposure to sib calls were incubated with more advanced embryos from Day 16 until Day 21. At that time they were moved to another incubator where they were exposed to prerecorded brooding-like sib calls (figure 5, chapter 2) for 55 minutes every other hour during Days 21 and 22. (As measured by a fast reading on Scale B of a B. & K. Precision Sound Level meter inside the incubator, the least intense notes

Fig. 13. Sound-attenuated incubators. Each egg is placed in individual compartment. Assistant holds one lid from each incubator to show details of lid construction. Incubators are heated by electrical heating wire. For the present experiments, peking duck eggs are placed in compartments on Day 23 (4 days before hatching) and hatchability is normal. Each compartment is opened every 4 to 6 hours during hatching process. The incubators are in a sound-attenuated room and air-conditioner fan motor provides a fairly constant background masking noise (73–75 dB). The incubator rooms are illuminated by black fluorescent lights.

peaked at 77 dB, the highest notes peaked at 89 dB, and most of the notes peaked at 81–82 dB.) Twenty-four of these embryos were tested to the mallard maternal call on Day 23 to determine if the premature exposure to sib vocalizations would accelerate the time of appearance of the increase in bill-clapping to the mallard call.

Fig. 14. Sound-attenuated incubator compartment with lid removed. Egg rests on recessed wire above water tray. Each compartment is fitted with loud speaker for stimulation experiments. (In the present work the sound-attenuated incubators were used only in connection with the isolation experiments.)

Results

As shown in table 25, the 38 embryos placed in auditory isolation on Day 23 did not show the usual increase in bill-clapping rate (or vocalization rate) when tested with the mallard call on Day 24. When the performance of the embryos is examined according to whether they were tested on

TABLE 25

Change in Baseline Rate of Embryonic Bill Clapping in Response to Mallard Maternal Call on Day 24 as a Consequence of Decreased Exposure to Sib Peeping

Groups Tested	Number of Embryos Showing	
	Increase ($+$)	Decrease ($-$)
Normal control ($N = 20$)	16	4
Decreased exposure ($N = 38$)	19	19

NOTE: Fewer of the embryos in the decreased exposure group showed an increase in bill-clapping in comparison to the normal control group (Chi-Square $= 3.75$; one-tailed $p < .05$).

the first half ($N = 21$) or last half ($N = 17$) of Day 24, there was no tendency toward increased bill-clapping to the mallard call in either subgroup. Another group of embryos which was isolated on Day 23 did not show the usual increase in bill-clapping to the mallard call even on Day 26 (previously published data, Gottlieb 1968b, p 169, table 3),

TABLE 26

Change in Baseline Rate of Embryonic Bill-Clapping in Response to Mallard Maternal Call on Day 23 as a Consequence of Enhanced Exposure to Sib Peeping on Days 21–22

Groups Tested	Number of Embryos Showing	
	Increase ($+$)	Decrease ($-$)
Normal control ($N = 25$)	4	21
Enhanced exposure ($N = 24$)	11	13

NOTE: More of the embryos in the enhanced exposure group showed an increase in bill-clapping in comparison to the normal control group (Chi-Square $= 3.82$; one-tailed $p < .05$).

On the other hand, as indicated in table 26, the embryos which received premature exposure to the prerecorded vocalizations of sibs on Days 21 and 22 showed a statistically reliable tendency to increase their bill-clapping rate when exposed to the mallard call on Day 23. Under usual conditions there is a decrease in bill-clapping in response to the mallard call on Day 23, with the increase appearing initially on Day 24 of embryonic development.

Discussion

The present results indicate that the decrease in bill-clapping rate in response to the maternal call on Day 23, and the increase on Day 24, is related to the amount of auditory stimulation typically encountered during the final stages of embryonic development. When the embryos are prematurely exposed to the vocalizations of sibs on Day 21 and 22, they begin to show an increase in the bill-clapping response on Day 23. On the other hand, when they are kept from hearing the vocalizations of sibs, the embryos do not show the usual increase in bill-clapping to the mallard call on Day 24 or even on Day 26.

These results indicate that the changes in the bill-clapping response to the maternal call do not go through an invariable, predetermined course which is entirely a function of organic maturation. Rather, the changes beyond Day 22 of embryonic development are intimately related to the usual amount of auditory stimulation provided by communal incubation. In this sense, the usual course of change in the bill-clapping response to the mallard call beyond Day 22 can be said to be a probabilistic phenomenon — the timing and schedule of changes in the bill-clapping response are a joint function of the maturational stage of the embryo and the amount of stimulation to which the embryo is normally exposed during the developmental process. The current evidence thus provides some further support for the idea that normally occurring sensory stimulation plays a regulative role in the ontogeny of embryonic behavior (Gottlieb 1968b).

While the usual behavorial sign (+ in bill-clapping) associated with the embryo's ability to respond selectively or discriminatively to the mallard call on Days 24 and 26 was absent in the isolated embryos, the discriminative ability of the isolated embryos was not the primary issue of the present experiments. The main question in this regard is the effect of normally occurring prenatal stimulation on postnatal perception — the embryonic effects may be entirely transitory or, at best, restricted to the embryonic period. Therefore, the question of the influence of the normal amount of embryonic sensory stimulation on the further development of the embryo's species-specific discriminative ability is best answered by the experiments in the next chapter (10), where birds which have had varied amounts of prenatal auditory experience are placed in simultaneous auditory choice tests at various times after hatching. (Discussion of the embryo's ability to respond selectively to the mallard call on Day 22, in advance of exposure to the vocalizations of self or sibs, is reserved for chapter 10.)

Summary

By varying the amount and time of normally occurring auditory stimulation, it is possible to either accelerate or decelerate changes in the embryo's usual response to its maternal call. Thus, the peking duck embryo's response to its maternal call on Days 23 to 26 does not go through an invariable, predetermined course which is solely a result of organic maturation. The embryo's response on each of these days is probabilistically determined by its maturational stage and the amount of stimulation which it normally encounters.

10

The Bearing of Normally Occurring Auditory Stimulation on the Duckling's Postnatal Discrimination of Its Maternal Call

ON the basis of the data presented in the preceding two chapters, we know that the peking duck embryo can respond discriminatively to the maternal call of its species as early as Day 22 (five days before hatching), and that this initial capability arises in advance of hearing its own vocalizations or those of more highly developed embryos. When the embryo's subsequent exposure to such stimulation (sib vocalizations) is either augmented or reduced, the typical course of the embryo's response to the maternal call is altered. The crucial question is whether these alterations are carried over into postnatal behavior, as evidenced by a heightened or reduced responsiveness to the maternal call, or an increased or decreased ability to discriminate the maternal call — and that question is the subject of the present experiments. Thus, from the standpoint of the interrelationship of prenatal sensory stimulation and postnatal perception, the experiments presented in this chapter are the most relevant ones in the monograph. The normally occurring auditory experience of the birds has been manipulated in a graded series of experiments ranging from virtually no prenatal or postnatal auditory stimulation to an experimentally defined normal amount of prenatal and postnatal auditory stimulation.

Experiment I
Effect of Prenatal Auditory Deprivation on the Postnatal Auditory Discrimination of the Mallard vs. Wood Duck Maternal Calls

While it is of importance to know that the embryo's response to the mallard call is affected by increasing and decreasing the amount of normally occurring prenatal auditory stimulation, a much more significant question concerns the effect of such stimulation on the bird's postnatal response to the mallard call. Is it essential for the embryos to hear their own vocalizations in order to be able to discriminate the mallard call after hatching? The clearest way to answer that question is to deprive the embryos of hearing their own vocalizations and to test their discriminative ability after hatching. Thus, the present experiments examine the postnatal auditory discriminative perception of embryos which have been devocalized and incubated and brooded in individual isolation. The behavior of the devocalized ducklings is compared to the behavior of sham-operated (vocal) ducklings which have been incubated and brooded in individual isolation. The performance of the latter group is compared to unoperated ducklings which have been incubated and brooded under the same conditions.

Method
All the embryos were incubated in a forced-draft incubator in a sound-shielded room until Day 23, at which time they were placed in the individual sound-attenuated compartments described in chapter 9. Prior to Day 23 none of the embryos was exposed to the vocalizations of more advanced embryos or hatchlings. After Day 23 the sham-operated and unoperated vocal-isolates could hear their own

vocalizations; and, since the compartments were not absolutely sound-proof, in some instances they might have heard an occasional loud vocalization produced by a bird in another compartment. Since the devocalization procedure absolutely mutes only around 90% of the embryos, the same possibility held for the devocal-isolates. In the latter case, however, the amount of vocalizations that the devocal embryos could have heard was further reduced by the fact that a very small proportion of these embryos could vocalize.

The embryonic devocalization procedure has been described fully by Gottlieb and Vandenbergh (1968). It involves making an incision in the skin over the syrinx and coating the underlying tympaniform membranes with nonflexible collodion (40 gr. pyroxylin, 750 ml. ethyl oxide, and 250 ml. ethyl alcohol). Collodion is used in hospitals as a surgical dressing, and it is nontoxic. The substance dries almost instantaneously and rigidifies the tympaniform membranes so that they can not vibrate. When the tympaniform membranes are made rigid, the embryo and hatchling are prevented from vocalizing. As previously documented (Gottlieb and Vandenbergh 1968, pp. 320–21), the devocalization procedure has no untoward effects on hatchability. A devocalized and a nonoperated duckling are shown in figure 15.

In the present experiments, an explicit attempt was made to devocalize the embryos during the "tenting" stage, that is, shortly before their bill penetrated into the air space at the large end of the egg (Day 24–25), well in advance of "pipping" the shell. Pipped eggs were excluded, and no embryo older than Day 25, 12 hours was included. Since it is only a matter of a few hours between the time of tenting and penetration into the air space, we failed to catch all of the embryos during the tenting stage and these were devocalized shortly after their bill had penetrated into the air space. The purpose of allowing the embryo to reach the tenting stage before devocalization was to increase hatchability. By the time the embryo's bill begins to push against the chorioallantoic and inner-shell membranes, giving a tent-like appearance to the membranes, pulmonary respiration is usually established. If embryos are exposed before that time, whether they are subjected to the devocalization procedure or not, the probability of hatching is severely reduced (Gottlieb and Vandenbergh 1968, p. 321). The disadvantage of waiting till pulmonary respiration has started

FIG. 15. Devocalized duckling (left) and vocal duckling (right). The scar from the incision can not be seen without removing the down from the duckling's chest. The bodily growth and development of the devocalized ducklings appear to be normal; the ducklings usually regain their vocal ability within a few months after hatching (Gottlieb and Vandenbergh 1968).

125

is that the embryos usually vocalize when being handled during the operation. It turns out that this meagre amount of auditory stimulation has no measurable effect in the discrimination test after hatching (data presented in "Results"). In our hands the complete operation typically takes 15 minutes or less.

The postnatal performance of the devocalized embryos is to be compared with sham-operated embryos, and the sham-operated embryos are to be compared with non-operated embryos, with all embryos being incubated and brooded under the same conditions. The sham-operated embryos were treated like the devocalized embryos, with the exception that no actual coating was applied to the tympaniform membranes. A number of substitute substances were applied to the tympaniform membranes for the sham operation; however, all the substances produced partial devocalization. Flexible collodion, for example, was almost as effective as nonflexible collodion. A mixture of ethyl oxide and ethyl alcohol, without the usual pyroxylin coating base of collodion, also partially devocalized the embryos. Petroleum jelly (Vaseline) caused some qualitative ("scratchy") changes in the embryo's vocalization. Finally, it was decided to merely pass a brush (without any collodion on it) over the tympaniform membranes, in the same way that collodion is applied to the membranes of the devocalized embryos. The embryos so treated constituted the sham-operated control group. All of these embryos could vocalize normally. The nonoperated control embryos were not removed from their individual compartments at any time, except at hatching, when all the ducklings in each of the three groups were moved to individual sound-attenuated brooder compartments where they remained until the time of testing.

While the devocalization or sham operation does not affect hatchability, it does affect the length of the incubation period. The embryos which are pulled partially out of the shell either for devocalization or the sham operation hatch sooner than the nonoperated embryos (in which the egg has not been opened). Including 77 devocalized and 62 non-operated birds for other experiments, the mean incubation time was 26 days, 16 hours for the devocalized embryos (range: 25 days, 17 hours to 27 days, 18 hours) and 27 days, 1 hour for the nonoperated embryos (range: 26 days, 14 hours to 27 days, 22 hours). This difference in incubation duration is reliable ($p < .00003$), and it does affect the developmental age of the groups at testing. All the birds were tested between 15 to 31 hours after hatching, with a mean posthatch age of 23 hours in the devocalized group, 25 hours in the sham-operated group, and 24 hours in the nonoperated group. The respective mean developmental age of the three groups at testing was 27 days, 17 hours (devocal), 27 days, 12 hours (sham), and 28 days, 9 hours (unoperated). The eggs in the nonoperated control group were not opened so the embryos hatched at the usual time (later than the operated embryos). Thus, the unoperated embryos had the advantage of being somewhat older (and, presumably, stronger) at the time of the test, in addition to any advantage accruing from the complete absence of any prior physical disruption (opening the egg and surgical interference).

Results

As can be seen from the ducklings' preference in the mallard vs. wood duck call choice test in table 27, the devocal-isolates' discrimination of the mallard call was inferior to the performance of the sham-operated group ($p = .05$) and the unoperated group ($p = .05$); the sham-operated group's discrimination of the mallard call was perfect, as was the unoperated control group. While the discriminative ability of the devocal-isolates was poor compared to the other groups, the devocal-isolates as a group did discriminate the mallard from the wood duck call: 19 chose the mallard call and 6 chose the wood duck call (Binomial Test, $p = .01$).

As shown in table 28, the devocal ducklings responded more slowly (longer latency) to the mallard call than the birds in the other groups. There were no differences between the sham-operated ducklings and the unoperated ducklings in latency or duration of response to the mallard

TABLE 27

Preference of Twenty-Four–Hour–Old Unoperated, Sham-Operated, and Devocal-Isolated Ducklings in Mallard vs. Wood Duck Maternal Call Choice Test during Five-Minute Auditory Approach Test

Condition	N	Responded %	Mallard	Wood Duck	Both
Unoperated vocal-isolated	39	54	21	0	0
Sham-operated vocal-isolated	31	68	21	0	0
Operated devocal-isolated	44	59	19	6	1

NOTE: No difference in preference between sham and unoperated groups. Devocal group preference for the mallard call was less than the sham ($p = .05$) and unoperated ($p = .05$) groups. Devocal group preference for mallard call was greater than their preference for wood duck call (Binomial Test, $p = .01$), however.

call. As could be anticipated from the ducklings' preference (table 27), the devocal group showed a stronger response (shorter latency and longer duration of response) to the wood duck call than the birds in the other groups (p values reported in note to table 28).

The devocalization procedure on Day 24 takes 10 to 15 minutes and many of the embryos vocalized during the operation. To determine if this small amount of auditory experience was in any way related to the devocal ducklings' performance in the choice test on Day 27, a rank-order correlation coefficient was computed between the number of vocalizations emitted during the operation (0–62 vocalizations) and the duration of the devocalized ducklings' response to the mallard call (14–245 secs.), and there proved to be no relationship between these two variables ($rho = .11$). We further analyzed the discrimination performance of the devocalized ducklings which vocalized only once or not at

TABLE 28

Latency and Duration of Response of Twenty-Four-Hour-Old Unoperated, Sham-Operated, and Devocal-Isolated Ducklings in Mallard vs. Wood Duck Maternal Call Choice Test during Five-Minute Auditory Approach Test

Condition	N	Latency (sec.)				Duration (sec.)			
		Mallard		Wood Duck		Mallard		Wood Duck	
		M	S.D.	M	S.D.	M	S.D.	M	S.D.
Unoperated vocal-isolated	39	76.7	73.7	300.0	0.0	169.9	76.2	0.0	0.0
Sham-operated vocal-isolated	31	58.5	55.8	274.0	82.0	177.2	76.3	1.8	5.7
Operated devocal-isolated	44	137.4	111.8	237.5	94.8	128.6	102.9	25.9	48.9

NOTE: No difference in latency and duration to mallard call between sham and unoperated groups. Longer latency of devocal group to mallard call differs reliably from sham ($p = .008$) and unoperated ($p = .04$). No difference in duration of response to mallard call between any of the groups. Devocal group had a shorter latency and longer duration to wood duck call than sham (latency $p = .08$; duration $p = .004$) and unoperated ($p = .04$; $p < .0006$).

129

all during the operation to determine if they were the ones which failed to discriminate. Of 10 such birds, 5 chose the mallard call, 1 chose the wood duck call, and 4 did not respond, thereby indicating that this group did not contribute disproportionately to the 7 devocal birds which failed to discriminate (6 ducklings chose the wood duck call and 1 duckling showed no preference). Thus, both the correlation coefficient and the last analysis indicate that the small amount of auditory experience which the embryo did or did not get during the devocalization procedure is not measurable in its postnatal test performance. (As will be seen in Experiment II, if the embryo is allowed more opportunity to aurally stimulate itself by delaying the usual time of devocalization, a profound effect is observed in its postnatal test performance.)

All the birds were tested around 24 hours after hatching. After the test each bird was returned to its isolation compartment to await a second test with the mallard and wood duck calls at 48 hours after hatching. In the second test the calls were interchanged between the speakers to prohibit a response based simply on position; in effect if the bird was to again approach the same call, it would have to now go to the side of the apparatus opposite to its previous response. To further preclude the possibility that the bird might return to the familiar visual area of the apparatus in advance of the calls being emitted from the speakers, the speakers were activated within 3 to 4 seconds after the bird was placed in the apparatus, rather than adhering to the usual 10 to 15 second delay.

It was possible to retest only 30 of the devocal ducklings, 19 of the unoperated vocal-isolated ducklings, and 18 of the sham-operated ducklings. As shown in table 29, almost all of the devocal ducklings which had chosen the wood duck call in the first test responded to the mallard call in the second test. In all of the groups a large majority of the ducklings which had responded to the mallard call in the first test continued to do so in the second test. These results suggest that the relatively poor performance of the devocal ducklings (i.e., the ones which chose the wood duck call) in the first test simply reflected a delay in the manifestation of their ability to discriminate the mallard and wood duck

TABLE 29

Preference of Devocal-Isolated, Vocal-Isolated, and Sham-Operated Ducklings in Retest at Forty-Eight Hours (Mallard vs. Wood Duck)

	Mallard	Wood Duck	Both	Neither
DEVOCAL-ISOLATED				
1st Test (24 hrs.)	13	5	1	11
2d Test (48 hrs.)				
Mallard	8	4	0	4
Wood duck	1	0	1	0
Both	1	0	0	0
Neither	3	1	0	7
VOCAL-ISOLATED				
1st Test (24 hrs.)	11	0	0	8
2d Test (48 hrs.)				
Mallard	11			1
Wood duck	0			0
Both	0			1
Neither	0			6
SHAM-OPERATED				
1st Test (24 hrs.)	14	0	0	4
2d Test (48 hrs.)				
Mallard	13			3
Wood duck	0			0
Both	0			0
Neither	1			1

NOTE: All of the birds were not retested; the numbers under each column for the 1st test at 24 hrs. refer only to the ducklings which were retested at 48 hrs.

calls. In order to substantiate this interpretation, another experiment like the one above was performed. Forty-eight embryos were devocalized, isolated, and given their initial test with the mallard vs. wood duck calls at 48 hours after hatching instead of 24 hours after hatching. (The actual mean posthatch age at testing was 48 hours, while the mean developmental age was 28 days, 18 hours.) If the performance of the devocal ducklings at 24 hours of age merely reflected a delay in the manifestation of their ability to discriminate the mallard call, the present devocal ducklings should discriminate more or less perfectly at 48 hours. As shown in table 30, the prediction was verified — the devocal-

TABLE 30

Preference of Twenty-Four–Hour–Old and Forty-Eight–Hour–Old Devocal-Isolated Ducklings in Mallard vs. Wood Duck Maternal Call Choice Test during Five-Minute Auditory Approach Test

Age (hrs.)	N	Responded %	Preference (N) Mallard	Wood Duck	Both
Twenty-four	44	59	19	6	1
Forty-eight	48	63	29	0	1

NOTE: Devocal ducklings tested at 48 hrs. after hatching showed a greater preference for the mallard call than the devocal ducklings tested at 24 hrs. ($p = .02$).

isolated ducklings initially tested at 48 hours discriminated the mallard call reliably better ($p = .02$) than the devocal-isolated ducklings initially tested at 24 hours. The older ducklings also responded more promptly (latency) to the mallard call than the younger ducklings (table 31). The younger devocal ducklings responded more strongly to the wood duck call (shorter latency and longer duration of response) than the older ducklings (p values in note to table 31).

Discussion

Ducklings which have been almost completely prevented from hearing their own vocalizations or those of sibs are able to discriminate the mallard maternal call from the wood duck maternal call in a simultaneous auditory choice test

TABLE 31

Latency and Duration of Response of Twenty-Four-Hour-Old and Forty-Eight-Hour-Old Devocal-Isolated Ducklings in Mallard vs. Wood Duck Maternal Call Choice Test

Age (hrs.)	N	Latency (sec.)				Duration (sec.)			
		Mallard		Wood Duck		Mallard		Wood Duck	
		M	S.D.	M	S.D.	M	S.D.	M	S.D.
Twenty-four	44	137.4	111.8	237.5	94.8	128.6	102.9	25.9	48.9
Forty-eight	48	77.0	75.7	294.2	32.0	156.0	84.5	2.4	13.3

NOTE: 48-hour-old ducklings had shorter latency to mallard call ($p = .04$). No difference between groups in duration of response to mallard call. The 24-hour-old group responded more promptly ($p < .001$) and longer ($p < .001$) to the wood duck call than the 48-hour-old group.

at 24 hours after hatching. At this time, however, their discrimination of the mallard call is not as highly perfected as ducklings which have been allowed to hear their own vocalization (sham-operated vocal-isolates). The sham-operated ducklings discriminated the mallard call as perfectly as unoperated ducklings at 24 hours after hatching. Thus, it is not the surgical interference as such which caused the devocalized ducklings to be less apt to discriminate the mallard call at 24 hours after hatching. Rather, the deficiency can be attributed to the lack of exposure to some (unknown) amount of normally occurring auditory stimulation. Therefore, if the duckling is to exhibit the usual capability of discriminating the mallard call from the wood duck call at 24 hours after hatching, it must be exposed to some amount of normally occurring auditory stimulation. With respect to the mallard vs. wood duck call choice test, the auditory deprivation introduces a lag in the development of the usual discriminative ability of the duckling. This is evidenced by the devocal-isolates' manifest ability to perfectly discriminate the mallard from the wood duck call at 48 hours after hatching. The improvement in performance of the ducklings which were given their first test at 48 hours, as compared to the performance of the 24-hour-old ducklings, also rules out the possibility that the 24-hour-old devocal-isolates performed relatively poorly because of partial deafness incurred by auditory deprivation; that is, if the devocal-isolated birds tested at 24 hours after hatching were partially deaf, the devocal-isolates tested at 48 hours after hatching should have been equally as deaf, if not more so, since they were subjected to an additional 24 hours of auditory isolation.

The significance of the present finding for an ontogenetic theory of species-specific perception is that exposure to normally occurring stimulation helps to regulate the time of appearance of the perfected response, as well as the latency of the perfected response. Deprivation is associated with a longer latency of response and a later appearance of the perfected response. A certain amount of exposure to normally occurring stimulation leads to a shorter latency of response and an earlier appearance of the perfected response. Thus, normally occurring stimulation operates to lower the threshold of the perfected response, and it is responsible for the perfected response appearing at the normal or usual time after hatching.

Experiment II
Effect of Prenatal Auditory Deprivation on the Postnatal Auditory Discrimination of the Mallard Maternal Call in Various Other Test Situations
The devocal-isolated ducklings were able to discriminate the mallard call from the wood duck call perfectly at 48 hours after hatching. In the present experiment, we will examine the discriminative ability of devocal-isolated ducklings in various simultaneous choice tests: mallard vs. duckling (sib) call, mallard vs. pintail maternal call, and mallard vs. chicken maternal call. The incubation, devocalization, and isolation procedure was exactly the same as that employed in the previous experiment. To avoid the delay factor found in the mallard vs. wood duck test, all the present groups were tested at 48 hours after hatching instead of 24 hours. The actual mean posthatch age in all the groups was either 47 or 48 hours, and the mean developmental age was Day 28, 13 hours for the mallard vs. duckling test, Day 28, 17 hours for the mallard vs. pintail test, and Day 28, 21 hours for the mallard vs. chicken test.

Results
As shown in table 32, the devocal-isolated ducklings were able to discriminate the mallard maternal call almost perfectly when it was in opposition to the duckling (sib) call or the pintail maternal call. The devocal-isolates were unable, however, to discriminate the mallard call in the mallard vs. chicken maternal call test.

With regard to latency and duration of response (table 33), in the mallard vs. duckling and mallard vs. pintail call tests, the ducklings showed highly reliable differences (favoring the mallard) in both the latency and duration of their response ($p < .00006$ in all cases). In the mallard vs. chicken

---

TABLE 32

Preference of Forty-Eight–Hour–Old Devocal-Isolated Ducklings in Various Simultaneous Auditory Choice Tests during Five-Minute Auditory Approach Test

Choice Test	N	Responded %	Preference (N) Mallard	Other	Both
Mallard vs. duckling	30	70	20	1	0
Mallard vs. pintail	27	74	20	0	0
Mallard vs. chicken	42	52	12	9	1

NOTE: In the mallard vs. duckling test and the mallard vs. pintail test, the preference was reliably greater for the mallard call in both tests (Binomial Test, $p<.002$). In the mallard vs. chicken test, the preference for the mallard call was not reliably greater than the preference for the chicken call (Binomial Test, $p>.05$).

---

call test, the ducklings did not show any differences in the latency and duration of their response to the mallard and chicken calls.

In view of the improvement in discrimination shown by the devocal ducklings in the mallard vs. wood duck test between 24 and 48 hours after hatching (previous experiment), 35 of the 42 devocal ducklings exposed to the mallard vs. chicken test at 48 hours were retested at 60 hours after hatching. As shown in table 34, the discrimination of the mallard call was still unreliable at 60 hours after hatching (11 birds chose the mallard call, and 5 birds chose the chicken call; Binomial Test, $p > .10$). An insufficient number of the ducklings in the mallard vs. duckling and mallard vs. pintail tests were retested; so, for comparison, the retest performance of devocal ducklings from the 48-hour mallard vs. wood duck call test is shown in table 34. As can be seen, these ducklings were still showing a highly reliable

TABLE 33

Latency and Duration of Response of Forty-Eight-Hour-Old Devocalized-Isolated Ducklings in Simultaneous Auditory Choice Tests during Five-Minute Auditory Approach Test

| | | Latency (sec.) | | | | Duration (sec.) | | | |
| | | Mallard | | Other | | Mallard | | Other | |
Test Calls	N	M	S.D.	M	S.D.	M	S.D.	M	S.D.
Mallard vs. duckling	30	80.3	79.4	291.4	39.5	182.9	92.2	3.0	13.8
Mallard vs. pintail	27	83.5	72.2	285.5	64.8	162.2	84.8	0.5	2.5
Mallard vs. chicken	42	67.2	127.9	204.1	110.6	67.5	92.8	33.7	57.7

NOTE: See table 32.

The ducklings in the mallard vs. chicken test showed no statistically reliable differences in their response to the mallard and chicken calls. Ducklings in mallard vs. chicken test had a longer latency to the mallard than the ducklings in the pintail ($p = .003$) and duckling tests ($p = .001$). Ducklings in mallard vs. duckling and mallard vs. pintail tests showed a longer duration of response to the mallard call than ducklings in the mallard vs. chicken test ($p < .003$ in both cases). Ducklings in mallard vs. chicken test had a shorter latency and longer duration of response to the chicken call than the ducklings' response to the pintail and duckling calls in the other tests ($p < .003$ in each instance).

137

discrimination of the mallard call at 60 hours after hatching (25 chose the mallard call and 2 chose the wood duck call; Binomial Test, $p < .002$).

On the outside possibility that the devocalization operation itself was somehow interfering with the ducklings' ability to

TABLE 34

Preference of Devocal-Isolated Ducklings in Retest at Sixty Hours (Mallard vs. Chicken and Mallard vs. Wood Duck)

	Mallard	Chicken	Both	Neither
MALLARD VS. CHICKEN				
1st Test (48 hrs.)	9	6	1	19
2d Test (60 hrs.)				
Mallard	5	2	0	4
Chicken	3	1	0	1
Both	0	0	0	0
Neither	1	3	1	14

	Mallard	Wood Duck	Both	Neither
MALLARD VS. WOOD DUCK				
1st Test (48 hrs.)	27	0	1	19
2d Test (60 hrs).				
Mallard	19	0	1	6
Wood duck	2	0	0	0
Both	0	0	0	1
Neither	6	0	0	12

NOTE: Only the performance of the retested birds (60 hrs.) is shown at 48 hrs.

discriminate the mallard call from the chicken call at 48 hours after hatching, a sham-operated, vocal-isolated group ($N = 40$) was tested to the mallard vs. chicken call test at 48 hours after hatching. As can be seen in table 35, the sham-operated isolates were able to discriminate the mallard call (Binomial Test, $p = .03$), albeit imperfectly. The fact that the sham-operated birds could discriminate the mallard call, and the mute birds could not discriminate the mallard call, indicates that it is not the surgical procedure per se which caused the deficiency in the discriminative ability of the devocal ducklings. Rather, it is their inability to stimulate themselves aurally which causes the deficiency in later auditory perception. To further show the influence of the amount of prior auditory stimulation on performance in the mallard vs. chicken call test, a sham-operated, vocal-

TABLE 35

Preference of Forty-Eight–Hour–Old Devocal-Isolated, Sham-Operated, and Vocal-Communal Ducklings in Mallard vs. Chicken Call Choice Test during Five-Minute Auditory Approach Test

		Responded	Preference (N)		
Condition	N	%	Mallard	Chicken	Both
Operated devocal-isolated	42	52	12	9	1
Sham-operated vocal-isolated	40	72	20	8	1
Sham-operated vocal-communal	43	70	26	6	1
Unoperated vocal-communal	30	80	24	0	0

NOTE: While the devocal-isolated ducklings did not show a preference between the mallard and chicken calls, the sham-operated isolates showed a preference for the mallard call over the chicken call (Binomial Test, two-tailed $p = .03$). The sham-operated isolates also showed a higher incidence of response than the devocal isolates ($p = .03$). A comparison of the sham-operated vocal-isolates with the sham-operated, vocal-communal ducklings indicates no difference in incidence of response or preference ($p > .05$ in both cases). There were no differences in the performance of the sham-operated, vocal-communal ducklings and the unoperated, vocal-communal ducklings in incidence of response or preference ($p > .05$ in both cases). Both vocal-communal groups showed a reliable preference for the mallard call over the chicken call (Binomial Test, two-tailed $p < .0008$ in both cases).

Based on the prediction that there will be an increase in responsiveness and discrimination as the amount of prior auditory stimulation increases, the p-values for comparisons between groups in this table and the next one are one-tailed, with the exception of comparisons between the two vocal-communal groups, in which the opportunity for prior auditory stimulation was the same.

communal group ($N = 43$) was also exposed to the mallard vs. chicken call test at 48 hours after hatching. As can be seen (table 35), the responsiveness of the sham-operated vocal-isolates and the sham-operated, vocal-communal ducklings was equally high; however, the sham-operated, vocal-communal ducklings showed a shorter latency and longer duration of response to the mallard call than the sham-operated, vocal-isolated ducklings (table 36). The

TABLE 36
Latency and Duration of Response of Forty-Eight-Hour–Old Devocal-Isolated, Sham-Operated, and Vocal-Communal Ducklings in Mallard vs. Chicken Call Choice Test during Five-Minute Auditory Approach Test

Condition	N	Latency (sec.)				Duration (sec.)			
		Mallard		Chicken		Mallard		Chicken	
		M	S.D.	M	S.D.	M	S.D.	M	S.D.
Operated devocal-isolated	42	167.2	127.9	204.1	110.6	67.5	92.8	33.7	57.7
Sham-operated vocal-isolated	40	137.4	114.6	233.7	103.2	83.8	86.4	25.3	55.1
Sham-operated vocal-communal	43	88.3	95.1	254.2	94.9	123.7	96.4	25.5	62.7
Unoperated vocal-communal	30	68.9	48.3	290.7	45.5	147.4	86.5	0.7	3.8

NOTE: Whereas the devocal-isolates did not show a reliable difference in the latency or duration of their response to the mallard and chicken calls, the sham-operated vocal-isolates showed a shorter latency ($p = .002$) and a longer duration ($p = .001$) of response to the mallard call than to the chicken call. Otherwise, there were no reliable differences between the two isolated groups in their response to the two calls. The sham-operated, vocal-communal ducklings showed a shorter latency ($p = .04$) and a longer duration of response ($p = .04$) to the mallard call than the sham-operated, vocal-isolated ducklings. There were no reliable differences between the sham-operated, vocal-communal ducklings and the unoperated, vocal-communal ducklings.

vocal-isolates, in turn, showed a higher incidence of response and better discrimination of the mallard call than the de-vocal-isolates (table 35).

To show once again that the minor surgery associated with the devocalization procedure does not in itself have an untoward effect on the birds' responsiveness and discrimination ability, the performance of an unoperated, vocal-communal group ($N = 30$) was compared to that of the sham-operated, vocal-communal ducklings in the mallard vs. chicken call test at 48 hours after hatching. The responsiveness and discrimination ability of these ducklings were no different than the sham-operated, vocal-communal ducklings (tables 35 and 36). These results clearly indicate that the surgical trauma associated with the devocalization operation does not in itself cause the poor performance of the devocalized-isolated ducklings. The present findings also show that the amount of prior auditory stimulation plays a critical role in determining the ducklings' response in the mallard vs. chicken call choice test.

While the above experiments do not allow any specific statement about the contribution of embryonic auditory stimulation per se to postnatal perception, another experiment we have performed does shed some light on this question. Namely, in one of our experimental replications of the devocal-isolates' performance in the mallard vs. chicken call test the standard procedure was changed in two ways: the upper limit of embryonic devocalization was raised from Day 25, 12 hours to Day 26, 0 hours and only those embryos were devocalized which had penetrated well into the air space. These two procedural variations allowed the embryos ($N = 32$) a much greater opportunity than usual to hear themselves vocalize before being muted. Specifically, in all of the previously reported experiments with muted or sham-operated ducklings the mean age at devocalization ranged from Day 24, 11–19 hours, whereas in the present experiment it was Day 25, 10 hours. Upon testing at 48 hours after hatching, these birds could discriminate the mallard call from the chicken call (17 chose the mallard call and only 1 chose the chicken call). Although in Experiment I in this chapter no relationship was found between the number of vocalizations the embryos emitted during the devocalization operation done at the standard age and their performance in the mallard call vs. wood duck call choice test, the present results with embryos which had a greater opportunity to hear themselves vocalize before being muted indicate the importance of embryonic auditory self-stimulation for the postnatal discrimination of the mallard call in the mallard vs. chicken call test. While further experiments are required to delineate the effectiveness of self-stimulation vs. stimulation from sibs and the importance of embryonic stimulation compared to postnatal stimulation, the results of the present experiment do show that prenatal auditory self-stimulation can contribute substantially to the duckling's postnatal discriminative response in the mallard vs. chicken call test.

Discussion
While the 48-hour-old duckling can discriminate the mallard maternal call from the duckling (sib) call, the pintail maternal call, and the wood duck maternal call in the absence of prior exposure to its own vocalizations or those of sibs, the duckling can not discriminate the mallard call from the chicken maternal call without the benefit of hearing its own vocalizations. Thus, in the latter case, exposure to normally occurring auditory stimulation is essential to the perfection of the auditory perceptual mechanism for species identification, while in the former instances the discrimination mechanism is perfected without the benefit of such stimulation. The most important conclusion here — the necessity of exposure to auditory stimulation for the perfection of species-specific perception — may be questioned on the grounds that if the mute-isolated ducklings which

142

failed to discriminate the mallard from the chicken maternal call at 48 hours of age had been tested at a later age, the deficiency would have been rectified as a consequence of further maturation. In defense of the conclusion, it can only be reiterated that these birds not only failed this particular test at 48 hours of age, but they showed no evidence of improvement in their discriminative ability when they were retested at 60 hours of age (see table 34).

TABLE 37

Two Acoustic Characteristics of Calls: Rate and Fundamental Frequency

Call	Rate (notes per sec.)	Fundamental Frequency (Hz)
Mallard maternal	4.1	1,125; 1,600
Duckling (sib)	4.4	3,400
Chicken maternal	2.5	775
Wood duck maternal	7.4	1,300
Pintail maternal	5.6	440

NOTE: In the discrimination experiments, the same burst of any given call is repeated at approximately 3-sec. intervals on the tape.

When the rate and fundamental frequency of the various calls are scrutinized (table 37), it becomes apparent why the ducklings can readily discriminate the mallard call from the duckling call and the pintail call: the fundamental frequency of these calls is radically different. While the wood duck call shares a fundamental frequency range with the mallard call, the rate of the two calls is very different, thereby providing a possible basis for discrimination. In the case of the chicken maternal call, both the rate and the fundamental frequency are more similar to the mallard call than are any of the other calls. From this way of analyzing the discriminative features of the calls, the duckling and pintail calls can be discriminated from the mallard call on the basis of frequency, while the wood duck call can be discriminated from the mallard call on the basis of rate. The chicken call is relatively difficult for the ducklings to discriminate from the mallard call because of the similarity in both frequency and rate. To gather some preliminary information on the basis upon which the ducklings discriminate the calls, an experiment was conducted (in collaboration with Marieta B. Heaton) in which the rate of the wood duck call was reduced to the same rate as the mallard call (4 notes per sec.) without altering the frequency of the wood duck call. (The rate of the wood duck call was reduced by inserting the appropriate amount of silent spaces between the various notes of the call.) If rate is the basis for the ducklings' usual discrimination of the two calls, in the present experiment

TABLE 38

Preference of Twenty-Four–Hour–Old Ducklings in Mallard vs. Wood Duck Maternal Call Choice Test with Rate-Altered Wood Duck Call (4 notes per sec.) during Five-Minute Auditory Approach Test

| Condition | N | Responded | Preference (N) | | |
			Mallard	Wood Duck	Both
Vocal-communal	28	21/28 = 75%	11	10	0

NOTE: The normal rate of wood duck call is 7.4 notes per sec., and the normal rate of the mallard call is 4.1 notes per sec. With the normal calls, the ducklings show a decided preference for the mallard call (cf. tables 14 and 27).

they should be unable to discriminate between them. As shown in tables 38 and 39, that is the case: normal, vocal-communal ducklings tested at 24 hours after hatching were unable to discriminate the mallard call from the wood duck call when the rate of the latter was equalized with the mallard call. Thus, in Experiment I in this chapter, where the devocal ducklings showed an imperfect discrimination of the mallard and wood duck calls at 24 hours after hatching, it can be tentatively assumed that the ducklings' inability to distinguish the rate of the two calls was responsible for their relatively poor performance. The rate of the most frequently emitted embryonic and neonatal vocalization (brooding-like call) is around 4 notes per second (table

TABLE 39

Mean Latency and Duration of Twenty-Four-Hour-Old Ducklings in Mallard vs. Wood Duck Maternal Call Choice Test with Rate-Altered Wood Duck Call (4 notes per sec.) during Five-Minute Auditory Approach Test.

Condition	N	Latency (sec.)				Duration (sec.)			
		Mallard		Wood Duck		Mallard		Wood Duck	
		M	S.D.	M	S.D.	M	S.D.	M	S.D.
Vocal-communal	28	159.8	110.7	208.1	111.8	78.0	104.3	69.8	91.9

NOTE: See table 3E.
No statistically reliable differences in latency or duration of response to mallard or wood duck calls.

1, chapter 2), thus exposure to this call may help to develop postnatal discriminations which are based on rate differences.

Similar experiments like the one above need to be carried out with the mallard and chicken calls in order to determine which aspects of the calls the ducklings use as the basis for discrimination. When this has been accomplished, it may be possible to make a much more definite statement on the specific contribution which normally occurring auditory stimulation makes in perfecting the duckling's auditory perceptual mechanism for species identification.[1]

As was shown in chapter 8, on Day 22 of embryonic development, two days in advance of hearing its own vocalizations or those of sibs, the embryo responds discriminatively to the mallard, wood duck, and chicken calls. The devocal-isolated ducklings were unable to discriminate the mallard and chicken calls after hatching, and they also showed a delay in their ability to discriminate perfectly between the mallard and wood duck calls after hatching. Thus, the auditory stimulation arising from the embryo's and hatchling's own vocalizations plays an important role in regulating the further development of the Day-22 embryo's auditory perceptual ability. We do not yet know which aspects of the maternal calls are essential to the embryo's discriminative response, nor do we know if these aspects are the same as those which are essential to the hatchling's discrimination of the calls on Day 27 or 28. It is necessary to have this information in order to be able to specify the exact contribution of normally occurring auditory stimulation to the postnatal discriminative abilities of the ducklings. With respect to the Day-22 embryos' discriminative abilities, to the extent that some quantitative feature of the calls is involved (e.g., rate or phrasing), it would be important to

1. At the present time (May 1969), Mrs. Marieta B. Heaton is engaged in an exhaustive analysis of the parameters which the embryos and hatchlings use to discriminate the mallard maternal call. The outcome of her investigation will shed much light on the matters discussed here.

push the macroscopic analysis further back in ontogeny to determine if any of the nonauditory rhythmic stimuli to which the embryo is exposed participate in the establishment of the embryo's auditory discriminative ability on Day 22. To the extent that frequency is the major basis for the embryo's discriminative response, it would be of great interest to examine the ontogenetic development of the frequency response of neural units in the embryo's auditory system. (The same sort of approach would also be desirable for rate.) The point is that the ontogenetic background of the duckling's ability to discriminate the maternal call of its species from other calls is susceptible to analysis and requires such analysis on at least two different levels (experiential and neurological) across a significant portion of the embryonic period. Also, the embryo's or duckling's capability to distinguish its maternal call from each of the other calls would appear to have a somewhat different ontogeny, according to whether the particular discrimination is made on the basis of frequency or rate. The devocalized-isolated ducklings could or could not discriminate the species call, depending on the acoustic characteristics of the calls which are placed in opposition to the mallard maternal call. The rate of the mallard maternal call seems to be a particularly important cue when the opposing call shares a fundamental frequency range with the mallard call. In other cases, the ducklings appear to be using frequency rather than rate. In any event, the ducklings do not appear to be reliant on only one aspect of the maternal call in order to discriminate it from other calls.

While it is extremely important to learn that the ducklings can discriminate the maternal attraction call of their own species from the maternal calls of certain other species in the almost complete absence of exposure to normally occurring auditory stimulation, it should be noted that their perception of the maternal call is not fully developed without such stimulation—the devocal-isolates could not discriminate the mallard and chicken maternal calls, while the vocal ducklings could make this discrimination. Thus, while the auditory perceptual mechanism for species identification eventually reaches a high degree of perfection without the benefit of exposure to normally occurring auditory stimulation, it does not reach full maturity under such conditions — exposure to a certain amount of normally occurring stimulation would appear to be essential to the complete development of the neonate's capacity for species identification. It is appropriate to emphasize "normally occurring stimulation" here because the ducklings have been deprived of hearing sounds to which they are ordinarily exposed in the usual course of events, and it is already known that not all sounds (or just any sounds at all) are capable of influencing their response. In previously published experiments (Gottlieb 1965a, table 2), it was found that prior exposure to the chicken maternal call led to a shorter latency and longer duration of the following-response to the mallard call, whereas prior exposure to the wood duck call did not appreciably affect the later following-response to the mallard call. Subsequently, it was shown that prior exposure to the duckling call improved both the approach- and following-response to the mallard call (Gottlieb 1966, tables 3 and 4).

Compared to vocal ducklings, the devocal ducklings showed four deficiencies in their response to the species maternal call. Specifically, the devocal-isolated ducklings showed a decreased incidence of response, a longer latency of response, a delay in the perfection of species-specific discrimination, and a failure to make a discriminative response in one of the tests. Because of the demonstrated contribution of normally occurring auditory stimulation in regulating the embryo's and hatchling's usual response to the maternal call of their species, it can be said that the epigenesis of species-specific perception is a probabilistic phenomenon and does not represent merely an unfolding of a fixed or predetermined organic substrate independent of normally occurring sensory stimulation. Fully normal, species-specific perceptual development grows out of exposure to stimulation typically encountered during ontogeny, and, in ducklings at least, this process begins prior to hatching.

According to the present results, natural selection, insofar as it has played a role in the evolution and maintenance of species-specific perception, would seem to have involved a selection for the entire developmental manifold, including both the organic and normally occurring stimulative features of ontogeny. That is, natural selection has been operating on birds which have had a certain ontogeny, and a normal constituent of that ontogenetic background has been the opportunity for certain kinds of function and the exposure to particular forms of stimulation. If that were not the case — that is, if normally occurring auditory stimulation was not playing a contributory role in the ontogeny of species-specific perception in the ancestors — when the usual auditory background is reduced in the ontogeny of the descendants, there should be no change in the species-specific maturation rate, threshold, and so on, in relation to species identification. Since these alterations did occur, as far as the ontogeny of species-specific perception is concerned, it can be said that natural selection has involved a selection for the entire developmental manifold (by which it is meant that sensory stimulative features are included as well as organic features). More traditionally stated, species-specific neural maturation or behavioral development is not only a consequence of genetic factors, but it is also a consequence of the characteristic developmental medium in or through which the genes operate. In the present case, one of the characteristic features of the developmental medium is the opportunity for auditory stimulation. At earlier stages there are undoubtedly other (more microscopic) features of the medium which are essential to the full realization of species-specific performance — it happens that here we are dealing with the more macroscopic features of ontogeny. Stated in this way, perhaps many investigators would agree that species-specific behavioral ontogeny represents a probabilistic outcome of the joint operation of various factors, among which is the bidirectional structure-function relationship. It is the task of developmental analysis to pinpoint the other factors which regulate the ontogenesis of species-typical behavior, eventually progressing from the neuromuscular and neurosensory levels of activity to the molecular domain.

With regard to the emphasis which we have placed here on the role of normally occurring stimulation in perfecting species-specific perception, it is pertinent to point out that the same condition may also hold for the development of species-typical motor behavior or action patterns. For instance, Fromme (1941), in his painstaking analysis of the development of swimming behavior in amphibians deprived of the usual opportunity for movement during the preswimming stage, found heretofore undetected deficiencies in their swimming ability. In a study of the development of normal locomotor patterns in amphibians deprived of sensory feedback, Weiss (1941, pp. 71, 74) noted deficiencies in postural control as well as imperfections in the execution of locomotor movements in animals whose limbs had been deafferented early in development. In a study of the development of singing ability in birds which had been deafened at various ages, Nottebohm (1968) found that the amount of deficiency in the adult song bore a systematic relationship to the time of deafening (the birds deafened earliest showed the greatest lack in the normal components of adult song). In addition, Nottebohm (p. 564) observed that deafened birds began singing their full song later than intact birds.

In the past it has been usual in sensory isolation or motor deprivation studies to ask merely whether the deprived animal could subsequently perform the species-typical behavior, not how well the animal could perform it. As we move into an era of increasingly sophisticated analyses of the development of behavior, it will not be altogether surprising to find that normally occurring sensory stimulation or motor movement is essential to the normal threshold, timing, and perfection of behavior conventionally regarded as instinctive or innate. If that prediction is fulfilled, the nature-nurture controversy may all but evaporate, and a consensus will have been reached on the idea that structure only fully realizes itself through function.

Summary
Embryos which have been devocalized and kept in auditory isolation show a delay in the perfection of their postnatal discriminative response to the species maternal call. Whereas sham-operated, vocal-isolated embryos show a perfect discriminative response to the mallard call in the mallard vs. wood duck call test at 24 hours after hatching, mute-isolated embryos do not show a perfect discriminative response to the mallard call in this test until 48 hours after hatching.

While the species-specific auditory discrimination ability of the devocal-isolated embryos eventually reaches a high degree of perfection at 48 hours after hatching, it does not reach full maturity — exposure to a certain amount of normally occurring stimulation would appear to be essential to the complete development of the neonate's capacity for species identification. Specifically, at 48 hours after hatching, the mute-isolated embryos are capable of discriminating the mallard call in simultaneous auditory choice tests involving the wood duck, pintail, and duckling calls, but they are unable to discriminate the mallard call from the chicken call at 48 hours or even 60 hours after hatching. As the embryos and hatchlings are permitted more and more exposure to normally occurring auditory stimulation in systematic increments, their response to the mallard call in the mallard vs. chicken call test improves in a step-wise manner. Sham-operated, vocal-isolates can discriminate the mallard call from the chicken call as can sham-operated, vocal-communal ducklings. The latter, however, show a shorter latency and longer duration of response to the mallard call. The sham-operated, vocal-communal ducklings respond as well to the mallard call as unoperated, vocal-communal ducklings, indicating that the surgery itself has no significant effect on the response of the ducklings.

11

Summary and Conclusions

THIS work has dealt with the question of how certain forms of birds come to identify members of their own species during the course of ontogeny. In pursuing the sensory and perceptual basis of species identification in young precocial birds, the contribution of maternal auditory and visual stimulation has been experimentally delineated, and the normal prenatal background of species-specific perception has been directly examined and manipulated.

In the postnatal experiments, young chicks and ducklings hatched in the laboratory have been exposed to the visual attributes of hens of various species and/or the attraction calls of hens of various species to determine the young birds' auditory and visual preferences and their ability to select the species-specific stimulus object. In the prenatal experiments, the embryos' ability to respond selectively to the species-specific maternal call has been investigated, with an emphasis on determining the normally occurring sensory stimulative factors which participate in the development and perfection of the embryos' and hatchlings' selective perception of the appropriate species maternal call without the benefit of prior exposure to maternal stimulation. Thus, all of the postnatal and prenatal experiments involved maternally naive birds.

Upon investigating the relative contributions of audition and vision to species identification during the early postnatal phase of development, it was found that species-specific maternal auditory stimulation is more potent than species-specific maternal visual stimulation in all species tested (domestic chicks, domestic ducklings, mallard ducklings, and wood ducklings). Thus, this generalization holds for domestic and wild forms as well as ground-nesting (mallard) and hole-nesting (wood duck) species. Since all the forms tested are precocial, it is not yet known whether this conclusion also holds for altricial species. The neonate's bias for the auditory component of the maternal stimulus configuration may be related to the fact that the auditory system begins functioning earlier in embryonic development than the visual system.

Upon analyzing the young birds' responsiveness to the maternal attraction calls of various species presented singly, it was found that the domestic chicks show the highest degree of species-specificity both in the approach- and the following-response. The ducklings approach a wider variety of calls than they will follow, and the following-response generally brings out the species-specificity of the birds' response. Tests with single calls indicate that domestication has not weakened the species-specificity of auditory perception, and hole-nesting ducklings do not show a higher degree of species-specific auditory perception than ground-nesting ducklings. At the methodological level simultaneous auditory choice tests (simultaneous presentation of maternal calls from two different species) are a more powerful way of determining the birds' ability to select the proper call than tests involving the presentation of only one call. The domestic chicks, domestic ducklings, and mallard ducklings show a very high ability to discriminate their maternal call under all simultaneous test conditions; under these test conditions, the hole-nesting wood ducklings are less able than the ground-nesting species to discriminate the maternal call of their own species.

No evidence for species-specificity of response was found when the ducklings were presented with only the visual attributes of the maternal parent. In addition, the normal or natural maternal audiovisual combination is not uniquely effective in eliciting the following-response of domestic and mallard ducklings. Other experiments showed that the relationship between the auditory and visual components of the maternal configuration is not strictly additive, so a knowledge of the independent effectiveness of each component does not allow one exactly to predict the relative strength of the ducklings' following-response when the two components are brought together as a unit. In general, however, the audiovisual combinations always provoke a stronger following-response than either component alone.

In analyzing the prenatal ontogeny of the ducklings' ability to respond discriminatively to the maternal call of its species, it was found that the peking duck embryo (domestic mallard form) becomes overtly responsive to the mallard maternal call on Day 22 (five days before hatching). At that time it is already able to respond selectively to the appropriate species maternal call, and this initial capability is not dependent on prior exposure to its own vocalizations or those of sibs. In experiments which manipulated the usual auditory experience of the embryo, variations in the amount and timing of normally occurring auditory stimulation predictably accelerated or decelerated changes in the embryo's usual response to its maternal call. Thus, the peking duck embryo's response to its maternal call on Days 23 to 26 does not go through an invariable, predetermined course which is solely a result of organic maturation. The embryo's response on each of these days is probabilistically determined by its maturational state and the amount of stimulation which it normally encounters.

In examining the prenatal background of the duckling's ability to respond discriminatively to the maternal call of its species after hatching, a number of significant points emerged. To answer the question of whether it is essential for the embryos to hear their own vocalizations in order to be able to discriminate the species maternal call after hatching, the final experiments examined the postnatal auditory discriminative ability of embryos which had been devocalized and incubated and brooded in individual isolation. First of all, these embryos showed a delay in the perfection of their postnatal discriminative response to the maternal call. Second, while the species-specific auditory discrimination ability of the mute-isolated embryos eventually reached a high degree of perfection after hatching, it did not reach full maturity — these ducklings were unable to make all the discriminations that vocal ducklings can make. Thus, exposure to a certain amount of normally occurring stimulation is essential to the complete development of the neonate's capacity for species identification.

The present results indicate that the epigenesis of species-specific auditory perception is a probabilistic phenomenon, the threshold, timing, and ultimate perfection of such perception being regulated jointly by organismic and sensory stimulative factors. In the normal course of development, the manifest changes and improvements in species-specific perception do not represent merely the unfolding of a fixed or predetermined organic substrate independent of normally occurring sensory stimulation. With respect to the evolution of species-specific perception, natural selection would seem to have involved a selection for the entire developmental manifold, including both the organic and normally occurring stimulative features of ontogeny.

With respect to the heavy emphasis placed here on the role of normally occurring stimulation in perfecting species-specific perception, it is pertinent to point out that the same condition may also hold for the development of species-typical action patterns. In the past it has been usual in sensory isolation or motor deprivation studies to ask merely whether the deprived animal can subsequently perform the species-typical behavior, not when or how well the animal performs it. As we move into an era of increasingly sophisticated analyses of the development of behavior, it will not be altogether surprising to find that normally occurring sensory stimulation or motor movement is essential to the normal threshold, timing, and perfection of behavior conventionally regarded as instinctive or innate. If this prediction turns out to be correct, the nature-nurture controversy may all but evaporate, and a consensus will have been reached on the idea that structure only fully realizes itself through function.

By way of concluding, it seems appropriate to place the present results in the broad theoretical context stated in the introductory chapter. One of the main questions in the ontogeny of behavior concerns the contribution of genetic (molecular) and other biochemical factors. While there is agreement that such factors provide an indispensable impetus to neural maturation, the exact nature or mechanics of the molecular and biochemical control of early neural maturation is not yet known. On the other hand, there is a basic theoretical disagreement on the contribution of function and sensory stimulation to normal or species-typical development which, at the level of neural maturation, concerns the unidirectionality or bidirectionality of the structure-function relationship.

Although the relationship of genetics to the ontogeny of species-specific behavior was not directly studied here, the species-specific auditory perceptual performances of chicks, peking ducklings, mallard ducklings, and wood ducklings described in the early chapters certainly provide indirect support for the general assumptions that (*a*) the genetic com-

157

plement sets (presently unknown) limits on behavioral development and (*b*) the species-specific genetic complement substantially increases the likelihood that the capability for certain forms of species-specific behavior will occur later in development. The latter statement does not, of course, specify the mechanisms whereby these capabilities are realized during ontogeny, but, rather, refers to the fact that the species-specific differences in auditory responsiveness to the various maternal calls are ultimately based on genetic differences between the species. The precise nature of such genetic differences is not known — this problem is in the future province of molecular biology. The third main assumption of modern conceptions of the development of behavior is that (*c*) intrinsic molecular and other biochemical processes provide an indispensable impetus for the early maturation of the nervous system. The present research (chapters 8, 9, 10) was conducted at such a late stage of embryonic development that the results do not bear directly or indirectly on this issue, though it is difficult to imagine how this particular assumption could possibly be mistaken (any more than the first two assumptions).

The main point of theoretical disagreement in behavioral embryology and in the development of behavior generally is the question of the contribution of normally occurring sensory stimulation or muscular movement to the ontogeny of species-typical behavior. The present results provide evidence that, during the late stages of embryonic development in ducklings, normally occurring auditory stimulation contributes both to the behavioral development of the embryo and the subsequent behavior of the hatchling. Other workers (Hamburger, Wenger, and Oppenheim 1966, Hamburger and Oppenheim 1967, Narayanan and Oppenheim 1968) find little or no evidence for the influence of sensory stimulation on the overt movements of chick embryos at either early or late stages of development, and their results also suggest discontinuities in the development of motor patterns such that later patterns are presumably in no significant way dependent upon the previous motility of the embryo. It has not been extensively investigated whether early sensory stimulation affects the maturation of the sensory systems in the chick embryo — such stimulation does affect the rate of maturation of the sensory systems in various species of newborn mammals (Gottlieb 1970) — or whether the threshold, timing and perfection of later motor patterns are in fact independent of previous muscular function. The latter is a most difficult question to answer with the chick because the artificial induction of even short-term paralysis results in serious skeletal abnormalities in the bird embryo (Drachman and Sokoloff 1966). As mentioned earlier, short-term paralysis of amphibian embryos prior to the free swimming stage results in quantitative deficiencies in their later swimming behavior (Fromme 1941), and early deafferentation also results in imperfections in postural control and locomotor movements in amphibians (Weiss 1941). That deficiencies should occur in the later locomotor movements of immobilized and deafferented animals is in keeping with the probabilistic viewpoint. The capability of young embryos to move in the absence of sensory stimulation, demonstrated by a number of investigators using a variety of vertebrate species (Corner 1964, Hamburger, Wenger, and Oppenheim 1966, Tracy 1926), in no way contradicts the potential significance of early motility and sensory stimulation for later behavior. The present experiments (chapters 9 and 10) indicate that embryonic sensory stimulation not only affects the development of behavior in the embryo, but that such stimulation also affects the behavior of the neonate.

In view of the very few studies available on the main questions of neural maturation and behavioral development, it is entirely up to future research to determine whether function commonly influences structural maturation and the ontogeny of species-typical behavior in various vertebrate forms, whether such an influence is present equally in all the sensory systems as well as the motor system, and, finally, how early in embryonic or fetal development such an influence is manifest. In this way we will eventually comprehend the relationship between molecular, biochemical, structural, functional, and sensory stimulative events in the ontogeny of behavior. It seems clear that our understanding of ontogenesis will benefit by pursuing the analysis of sensory and motor development to the earliest stages of embryonic motility and behavior.

References

Bateson, P. P. G.
1966. The characteristics and context of imprinting. *Biol. Rev.* 41:177–220.

Beach, F. A.
1955. The descent of instinct. *Psychol. Rev.* 62:401–10.

Boyd, H., and Fabricius, E.
1965. Observations on the incidence of following of visual and auditory stimuli in naive mallard ducklings (*Anas platyrhynchos*). *Behaviour* 25:1–15.

Brooks, W. D.
1902. The intellectual conditions for embryological science. II. *Science* 15:481–92.

Carmichael, L.
1927. A further study of the development of behavior in vertebrates experimentally removed from the influence of external stimulation. *Psychol. Rev.* 34:34–47.

Coghill, G. E.
1929. *Anatomy and the Problem of Behavior.* Cambridge University Press.

Collias, N. E.
1960. An ecological and functional classification of animal sounds. In *Animal Sounds and Communication* (W. E. Lanyon and W. N. Tavolga, eds.), pp. 368–91. Washington, D.C.: Intelligencer.

161

REFERENCES

Collias, N. E., and Collias, E. C.
1956. Some mechanisms of family integration in ducks. *Auk* 73:378–400.

Corner, M.
1964. Rhythmicity in the early swimming of anuran larvae. *J. Embryol. Exp. Morph.* 12:665–71.

Drachman, D. B., and Sokoloff, L.
1966. The role of movement in embryonic joint development. *Develop. Biol.* 14:401–20.

Fabricius, E.
1951. Zur Ethologie junger Anatiden. *Acta Zool. Fenn.* 68:1–178.

Fischer, G. J.
1966. Auditory stimuli in imprinting. *J. Comp. Physiol. Psychol.* 61:271–73.

Fromme, A.
1941. An experimental study of the factors of maturation and practice in the behavioral development of the embryo of the frog, *Rana pipiens. Genet. Psychol. Monogr.* 24:219–56.

Gottlieb, G.
1961. The following-response and imprinting in wild and domestic ducklings of the same species (*Anas platyrhynchos*). *Behaviour* 18:205–28.

1963a. A naturalistic study of imprinting in wood ducklings (*Aix sponsa*). *J. Comp. Physiol. Psychol.* 56:86–91.

1963b. Refrigerating eggs prior to incubation as a way of reducing error in calculating developmental age in imprinting experiments. *Anim. Behav.* 11:290–92.

1965a. Imprinting in relation to parental and species identification by avian neonates. *J. Comp. Physiol. Psychol.* 59:345–56.

1965b. Components of recognition in ducklings. *Nat. Hist.* 74: 12–19.

1966. Species identification by avian neonates: Contributory effect of perinatal auditory stimulation. *Anim. Behav.* 14:282–90.

1968a. Species recognition in ground-nesting and hole-nesting ducklings. *Ecology* 49:87–95.

1968b. Prenatal behavior of birds. *Quart. Rev. Biol.* 43:148–74.

1970. Ontogenesis of sensory function in birds and mammals. In *Biopsychology of Development* (E. Tobach, ed.). New York: Academic Press, (in press).

162

REFERENCES

Gottlieb, G., and Vandenbergh, J. G.
1968. Ontogeny of vocalization in duck and chick embryos. *J. Exp. Zool.* 168:307–26.

Gottlieb, G., and Simner, M. L.
1969. Auditory versus visual flicker in directing the approach response of domestic chicks. *J. Comp. Physiol. Psychol.* 67:58–63.

Gunther, W. C.
1965. Further observations on effect of nonoptimally high incubation temperature on frequency of pecking and color preference in the chick. *Indiana Acad. Sci.* 74:362–66.

Hamburger, V.; Balaban, M.; Oppenheim, R.; and Wenger, E.
1965. Periodic motility of normal and spinal chick embryos between 8 and 17 days of incubation. *J. Exp. Zool.* 159:1–14.

Hamburger, V., and Oppenheim, R.
1967. Prehatching motility and hatching behavior in the chick. *J. Exp. Zool.* 166:171–204.

Hamburger, V.; Wenger, E.; and Oppenheim, R.
1966. Motility in the chick embryo in the absence of sensory input. *J. Exp. Zool.* 162:133–60.

Hess, E. H.
1958. "Imprinting" in animals. *Sci. Amer.* 198:81–90.

1959. Imprinting. *Science* 130:133–40.

Holt, E. B.
1931. *Animal Drive and the Learning Process*, vol. 1. New York: Henry Holt.

Kear, J.
1965. The internal food reserves of hatching mallard ducklings. *J. Wildlife Mgmt.* 29:523–28.

Klopfer, P. H.
1959. An analysis of learning in young Anatidae. *Ecology* 40:90–102.

Kuo, Z-Y.
1967. *The Dynamics of Behavior Development.* New York: Random House.

Lehrman, D. S.
1953. A critique of Konrad Lorenz's theory of instinctive behavior. *Quart. Rev. Biol.* 28:337–63.

163

REFERENCES

Lockard, R. B.
1968. The albino rat: A defensible choice or a bad habit? *Amer. Psychologist* 23:734–42.

Lorenz, K. Z.
1940. Durch Domestikation verursachte Störungen arteigenen Verhaltens. *Z. angew. Psychol.* 59:2–82.

Marcström, V.
1960. Studies on the physiological and ecological background to the reproduction of the capercaillie (*Tetrao urogallus* Lin.). *Viltrevy* 2:1–69.
1966. Mallard ducklings (*Anas platyrhynchos* L.) during the first days after hatching. *Viltrevy* 4:341–70.

Narayanan, C. H., and Oppenheim, R. W.
1968. Hatching behavior in the chick embryo. II. Right-wing removal. *J. Exp. Zool.* 168:395–402.

Nottebohm, F.
1968. Auditory experience and song development in the chaffinch *Fringilla coelebs*. *Ibis* 110:549–68.

Oppenheim, R. W.
1968. Light responsivity in chick and duck embryos just prior to hatching. *Anim. Behav.* 16:276–80.

Oppenheim, R. W.; Jones, J. R.; and Gottlieb, G.
1970. Embryonic motility and posthatching perception in birds after prenatal gamma-irradiation. *J. Comp. Physiol. Psychol.* 71:6–21.

Porter, R. H., and Stettner, L. J.
1968. Visual and auditory influences on following responses of bobwhite quail (*Colinus virginianus*). *J. Comp. Physiol. Psychol.* 66:808–11.

Preyer, W.
1885. *Specielle Physiologie des Embryo.* Leipzig: Grieben.

Ramsay, A. O.
1951. Familial recognition in domestic birds. *Auk* 68:1–16.

Ramsay, A. O., and Hess, E. H.
1954. A laboratory approach to the study of imprinting. *Wilson Bull.* 66:196–206.

Schneirla, T. C.
1965. Aspects of stimulation and organization in approach/withdrawal processes underlying vertebrate behavioral development.

164

In *Advances in the Study of Behavior,* vol. 1, (D. S. Lehrman, R. A. Hinde, E. Shaw, eds.), pp. 1–74. New York: Academic Press.

1966. Behavioral development and comparative psychology. *Quart. Rev. Biol.* 41:283–302.

Sluckin, W.
1965. *Imprinting and Early Learning.* Chicago: Aldine.

Smith, F. V.
1969. *Attachment of the Young.* Edinburgh: Oliver & Boyd.

Smith, F. V., and Bird, M. W.
1963. The relative attraction for the domestic chick of combinations of stimuli in different sensory modalities. *Anim. Behav.* 11:300–305.

Sperry, R. W.
1965. Embryogenesis of behavioral nerve nets. In *Organogenesis* (R. L. DeHaan and H. Ursprung, eds.), pp. 161–86. New York: Holt, Rinehart, and Winston.

Tracy, H. C.
1926. The development of motility and behavior reactions in the toadfish (*Opsanus tau*). *J. Comp. Neurol.* 40: 253–369.

Tschanz, B.
1968. Trottellummen, Die Entstehung der persönlichen Beziehungen zwischen Jungvogel und Eltern. *Z. Tierpsychol.* suppl. 4, pp. 1–103.

Vince, M. A.
1968. Effect of rate of stimulation on hatching time in Japanese quail. *British Poultry Sci.* 9:87–91.

Weiss, P.
1941. Self-differentiation of the basic patterns of coordination. *Comp. Psychol. Monogr.* 17:1–96.

1955. Nervous system (neurogenesis). In *Analysis of Development* (B. H. Willier, P. A. Weiss, and V. Hamburger, eds.), pp. 346–401. Philadelphia and London: W. B. Saunders.

INDEX

Numbers in italics refer to page
on which figures (photographs) appear

audiovisual components, 46–47, 49; maternal auditory component, 47, 49, 51–52, 55, 63, 154; maternal visual component, 47, 49–52, 154; pintail call (single call test), 55–56, 58–60; wood duck call (single call test), 55–56, 58–60, 64; wood duck vs. chicken calls, mallard calls, and mandarin calls, 71–74

Yolk sac, nutritive value, 26